Mind Your Buckets!

"Be kind to one another."
– Ellen DeGeneres

Mind Your Buckets!

HOW TO UNDERSTAND, MANAGE, AND GROW YOUR CAPACITY FOR A HAPPIER LIFE

Jenny Battig, CHt

Jasten Publishing
Durham, North Carolina

ISBN: 978-0-9827190-4-6 (paperback)

Printed in the United States of America
Book design by Jenny Battig

Table of Contents

"We can't become what we need to be by remaining what we are."
– Oprah Winfrey

Introduction

Have you ever wondered why some days you can shrug off a challenge like a superhero, and other days, a tiny, spilled coffee feels like the end of the world? Or why some people seem to breeze through stress while you're ready to hibernate under a blanket with a hot cocoa while binge watching your favorite reality show? These aren't just random quirks of personality. They are the results of your unique internal system, you might think of it as your subconscious garden, quietly trying to keep things balanced and healthy so you don't experience drought conditions, or too much 'fertilizer' (i.e. shit!).

That frustrating feeling often comes from something deeper than just a bad day. For many of us, it boils down to that nagging little voice that whispers, 'You're just not good enough,' or 'You don't really deserve that.' And when that belief is humming in the background, life starts to look pretty unfair, doesn't it? We wonder why that person got the promotion, or why they seem to handle everything so effortlessly, while we're stuck feeling like we're constantly fighting upstream. That quiet ache? It often lives right in the gap between what we hoped for, what we expected, and the messy reality we're actually living. But what if I told you the secret to navigating that gap, and silencing those whispers, lies in understanding a hidden world of... buckets? Yeah, you heard me right. Buckets. And it's time to pull back the curtain to reveal a surprisingly simple, yet profoundly powerful, way to understand and navigate your emotional world: what I call the Emotional Bucket Balancing System, or EBBS.

Life, much like the ocean, is a constant cycle of ebbs and flows. There are times when everything feels expansive, effortless, and abundant – those are our 'flows.' And then there are periods of challenge, contraction, or feeling drained – our 'ebbs.' The good news is, by understanding your Emotional Bucket Balancing System (EBBS), you gain the practical tools to navigate these natural cycles. You learn not just to manage the emotional 'fills' and 'drains' of daily life, but also to address the deeper 'rocks' that might be holding you back, ensuring that even during life's 'ebbs,' you maintain your capacity for resilience, and during the 'flows,' you can truly ride the wave with Freedom, Lightness, Openness, Wellness, and Serenity (FLOWS). By the way, I'm a big fan of acronyms and metaphors, so bear with me.

So, what are these buckets, and why do they matter? Think of it this way: each of us carries a unique collection of emotional buckets, one for every kind of feeling or situation. There's a Sadness Bucket, an Anger Bucket, a Stress Bucket, even a Connection Bucket, and so on. The size of each bucket represents your personal capacity for that emotion or experience before it overflows. And here's the kicker: as illustrated in Figure 1, none of us come with labels on our foreheads showing the sizes of our buckets, or how full they're getting! That's why it's easy to misread ourselves and others. Your Anger Bucket might be super-sized, while your friend's can only hold a teacup's worth. And guess what? There's no shame in any bucket size. These capacities are unique, influenced by everything from your childhood experiences to old emotional baggage (you might think of those as big rocks taking up valuable space in your buckets!).

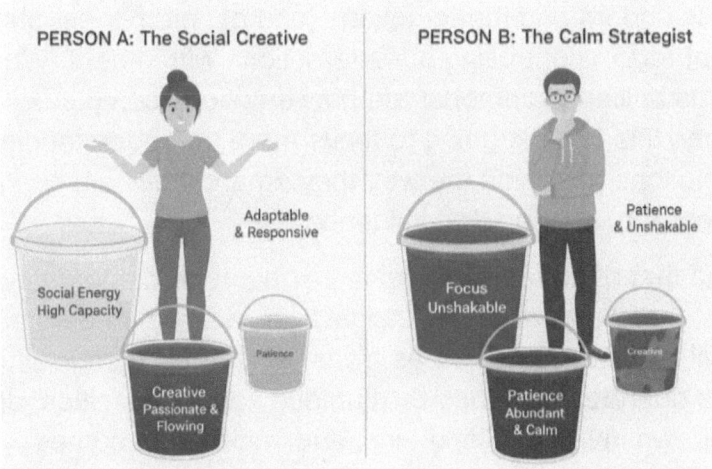

Figure 1 – Representation of the Variations in Emotional Buckets

This book isn't about judging your buckets, or anyone else's. Drawing from my experience over more than 10 years as a hypnotherapist, and my training in HeartMath and emotional intelligence, I've watched my clients' lives transform as they embodied the EBBS training. For the first time, I'm going to pull back the curtain on my proven signature system so you too can finally understand your own inner system, figure out what truly fills you up, what drains you dry, and how to spot when others are running on empty. By the time you finish, you'll be able to Mind Your Buckets! …creating a much happier life for yourself and those around you.

If you've ever seen the Pixar films in the Inside Out franchise, you probably remember the main characters were the various feelings that Riley had going on in her mind. They controlled her behaviors and responses to many of the things she was confronted with (like starting a new school or trying to make new friends). You might also recall that some of those characters seemed stronger than others. For example, Joy tried to run the show all the time, especially when Riley was little. And as a teenager, in Inside Out 2, Anxiety pushed Joy out of the way to take over Riley's responses. I absolutely love those movies because they do such a great job of helping us understand that emotions (and old memories) play a significant role in controlling our interactions with others. While those films brilliantly demonstrate how emotions can play off of each other, this book is going to focus more on understanding why those emotions push you the way they do and how you can affect them in order to change that influence.

In a world that often feels increasingly fragmented and defined by an 'us vs. them' mentality, the insights gained from understanding emotional buckets can serve as a vital bridge. By recognizing that everyone operates with their own unique set of capacities, dealing with their own invisible fills, drains, and 'rocks,' it becomes significantly easier to step out of judgment and into compassion and empathy. This metaphor is more than just a key to individual emotional awareness and regulation; it also holds the potential to help us remember our shared humanity, fostering greater understanding and connection even amidst our differences. It might just be an important key to helping us come back together.

There will always be differences between what you like and what others like, what's important to you vs what others find important (which can obviously even influence how we all vote), even what makes you feel comfortable and safe, as compared to what works to make others feel comfortable and safe. The message of this book isn't trying to change that, but keeping in mind that there are differences, and that's completely ok. In fact, understanding more about those differences might help explain why 'opposites attract' (to learn how to balance more of their buckets). Learning and applying the EBBS system from this book improves your emotional intelligence and gives you more control of your own capacities and behaviors, as well as making interactions with other people, who have different priorities and expectations, much easier.

Consider this your invitation to an exciting journey of self-discovery. We're going to dive into the hidden world of your emotional buckets, unearthing the mysteries of your capacity, understanding what truly fuels your well-being, and learning how to protect yourself from unnecessary emotional spills. I'm giving you a hands-on guide to mastering your internal system, allowing you to confidently Mind Your Buckets! ...and build a truly happier life for yourself and those around you. Let's get started!

"When we deny our emotion, it owns us. When we own our emotion, we can rebuild and find our way through the pain."
- Brené Brown

Chapter 1 Your Unique Set of Buckets

Alright, so we're peeking behind the curtain, and surprise! Instead of a powerful wizard pulling levers, like in Oz, what we find is actually a collection of... well, buckets. And guess what? We've all got 'em. Think of these as your personal emotional containers, each one designed to hold a certain amount of a particular feeling or experience. These aren't just for the 'Tough Stuff' like stress or anger, but also for those great things like joy, excitement, and connection. Every day, life throws things into these buckets, sometimes it's a gentle drizzle, sometimes it's a full-on downpour. The goal is to keep things balanced, so nothing unintentionally overflows or, just as importantly, runs completely dry.

Just so we're clear, I'm not suggesting there are literally buckets in your brain – or even small collection bins – but since it's easier to visualize something we've already seen before and our mind understands how it works, it's the best way I've come up with to help clients understand their uniqueness, as well as why other people may act a certain way. This approach really takes some of the pressure off when they compare what they can handle with what others seem to handle better. Many people fall into the trap of thinking if they feel overwhelmed by stress, anger, or depression, they've somehow failed as a human being. Sometimes that shows up in behaviors like smoking, drinking too much, over-eating, or other habits that almost seem like self-punishment since they aren't the most healthy choices. This feeling often gets worse when they see other people who don't appear to be overwhelmed by the same stuff.

One of the first things I share with people in that position is to realize that their bucket for handling stress (or anger, or anxiety, or whatever else) might just be smaller than someone else's. Or, perhaps it's already full of gunk from the past that they're still carrying around, which significantly diminishes their capacity to handle as much as they feel they 'should.' Think about it, would you expect a small watch battery to be able to provide enough power to run a car? No! Similarly, it's not practical to carry a car battery around on your wrist. They are both useful, we just have different expectations of them… and we can extend that concept to our emotional buckets.

Luckily, our buckets aren't exclusively about the 'Tough Stuff' we have to deal with in life... we also have them for the 'Good Stuff'! I know what you're thinking: your 'Tough Stuff' buckets, probably full of things like Frustration, Sadness, or Anxiety, sometimes block those 'Good Stuff' buckets, making it feel impossible to experience things like Joy, Fun, and Hope! Well, I totally get that feeling, and it's okay to acknowledge that that's exactly what it feels like. But maybe that's precisely why you picked up this book. It's here to help you realize you have way more control over those buckets than you ever imagined! We're gonna dive deeper into how this whole bucket system works: how you can increase your capacity, put limits on what goes into certain buckets, and keep things more balanced, giving you a better sense of 'Controo-ol!' (Sorry, I'm a Janet Jackson fan, so whenever I use that word, in my mind it sounds exactly like her song. Younger folks might just have to look that one up, lol.)

So, these buckets definitely aren't one-size-fits-all. Just like some people can have a couple sips of wine and feel a happy buzz, while others can finish a whole bottle and still be ready to solve the world's problems, our emotional buckets are unique to each of us. I've even worked with clients who were identical twins, but their buckets had developed much differently based on how they each felt they were treated as kids, all while growing up in the same household. Your Anger Bucket might be smaller than your sibling's, meaning you hit your limit quicker. Or your Anxiety Bucket might be super-sized compared to your best friend's, allowing you to handle more uncertainty before you start to spin.

The tricky part? These bucket sizes aren't etched on our foreheads for all to see. You can't just glance at someone and know if their Stress Bucket is bigger or smaller than yours, or if their Connection Bucket is bone dry. And honestly, there's no judgment here. Your capacity is simply your capacity, and it's heavily influenced by everything from your DNA to your life experiences. Heck, the sizes, shapes and colors of your buckets can even be influenced by factors beyond your direct control, such as brain chemistry, which can predispose you to certain emotional states; hormonal levels, which ebb and flow throughout life; or even generational trauma, which can subtly shape your emotional responses and sensitivities inherited from your ancestors. These aren't excuses, but simply acknowledgements that we all start with a unique emotional blueprint.

Sometimes, those buckets even have 'rocks' in them – old emotional baggage, past traumas, or those nagging 'not good enough' beliefs that take up valuable space, leaving less room for the good stuff and making it harder to handle the tough stuff. Maybe you've heard the analogy (or you can refer to the Figure 2 for a visual representation) about the jar full of rocks that people would say is 'full', but then a bunch of sand gets poured into the jar, filling gaps around the rocks, then people say, 'oh, NOW it's full', but then water is poured into the jar until it reaches the top, filling all excess space in the jar. Sometimes we don't realize how full our buckets are and assume the only way to fit more in is by getting a bigger bucket or an additional bucket, when removing some of those rocks can allow the sand to shift and settle, opening up much more capacity. Along those same lines, if we don't have good bucket maintenance, we may not even realize we still have a bunch of sand at the bottom of our bucket, which effectively reduces the working capacity for things that come up in our daily lives.

Figure 2 – Bucket with various 'fillers'

I'm pretty sure I'm not the ONLY one to snap a snide comment at someone because one of my buckets was overflowing. And if you're not super self-aware in moments like that, it's probably even more obvious when someone claps back at you or calls you a 'bitch,' leaving you internally thinking, 'Seriously?!' That reaction from them may mean they're reacting to your bucket overflowing, because your actions were different than they'd normally expect from you. Sometimes, a bucket overflowing can feel even more obvious for you, showing up as a panic attack, an ugly cry, sudden nausea, or a pounding headache.

These 'spills,' whether they manifest as a sharp word, a sudden burst of tears, or a physical symptom, are essentially signals from your system. They're not signs that you've failed as a human being; they're just your buckets screaming, 'I'm full!' Recognizing when these things are triggered by your emotional buckets is incredibly important. Because the best way to truly take care of what's causing those uncomfortable physical and emotional symptoms isn't always a pill or simply trying to ignore it. Often, it's by working directly on your buckets, which can lead to much more long-lasting relief with no unwanted side effects.

Our buckets aren't like concrete wells, set in stone forever. Think of it more like our clothes: the sizes can absolutely change as we grow and evolve. The biggest shifts in our bucket sizes usually happen early in life, shaped by those foundational experiences that determine how we see ourselves and what we feel worthy of. But here's the thing: our buckets can keep changing. Significant life experiences, whether we like it or not, can alter their capacity - sometimes making them bigger, sometimes shrinking them down. Becoming a parent often changes some of our buckets, for example, often expanding our bucket capacity of love or empathy for another human.

The good news is, we can also make conscious efforts to modify our buckets so we feel more balanced and in control. And you don't have to think of this as just a solo mission where only you are responsible. Your efforts can definitely get a boost from others, whether that's just asking for honest feedback and support from family, or reaching out to a professional like a therapist, hypnotherapist, or life coach.

In my own work, one of the things I've loved about doing hypnotherapy with clients is seeing how it helps them make those deep adjustments in just a few sessions, as long as they're truly open to and ready to do the work. While some people might think of hypnotherapy as being kinda 'woo woo', I can tell you, the more I've worked with it, the more logical and sensible it truly is. So many of our behaviors are influenced by our subconscious. Really, anything we don't have to consciously or intentionally do is a product of our subconscious (from breathing and growing hair, to our reaction to seeing a large spider in our house or even how we handle frustrating situations). Since hypnotherapy is basically just a method to speak directly to our subconscious to influence those responses and behaviors by bypassing the 'gatekeeper' analytical conscious mind that says, 'get outta here, we don't need to change nothin', the possibilities of what can be changed by influencing the subconscious are nearly endless!

A lot of that work that I do with clients in hypnotherapy is focused on helping them get those 'rocks' – those attachments to old emotional trauma – out of their buckets so they immediately have more capacity. And as we shift those self-limiting beliefs, we can also influence the overall size of the bucket itself. It's kinda like when we reach our adult clothing size, but then maybe we've 'bloated up' for whatever reason and decide to make a conscious effort (either on our own or with some external support) to fit back into our old, smaller clothes.

I've been talking about buckets and their capacities in general, but I want to get a little more specific. To truly start Minding Your Buckets, it helps to identify what kinds of emotional 'stuff' fills your various containers. Below, you'll find lists of common 'Tough Stuff' buckets, 'Good Stuff' buckets, and the 'Rocks' that can take up space. Take a moment to read through them. See which ones make you nod your head, which ones feel familiar, or which ones might surprise you. This is an invitation to self-discovery, helping you recognize your unique emotional landscape without judgment. And of course, this is not a comprehensive list by any means. You might even feel like some of these things make more sense to be combined in one bucket for you. Think of these lists as a general guide to the types of buckets different people may have (even if you don't have a bucket for some of these, someone else you interact with might be dealing with those buckets).

Examples of 'Tough Stuff' Buckets:

• Anger	• Annoyance	• Anxiety
• Boredom	• Confusion	• Depression
• Disappointment	• Discomfort	• Disgust
• Embarrassment	• Envy	• Exhaustion
• Fear	• Guilt	• Helplessness
• Hopelessness	• Hurt (emotional)	• Impatience
• Insecurity	• Loneliness	• Nervousness

Your Unique Set of Buckets

- Pain (physical)
- Reluctance
- Shame
- Suspicion
- Pessimism
- Resentment
- Shock
- Tension
- Regret
- Sadness
- Stress
- Worry

And examples of 'Good Stuff' buckets:

- Acceptance
- Affection
- Authenticity
- Calm
- Comfort
- Confidence
- Curiosity
- Energy
- Freedom
- Fun
- Honesty
- Independence
- Intelligence
- Love
- Optimism
- Peace
- Privacy
- Respect
- Self-esteem
- Talent
- Achievement
- Appreciation
- Balance
- Celebration
- Communication
- Connection
- Empowerment
- Enthusiasm
- Friendship
- Growth
- Hope
- Inspiration
- Involvement
- Meaning
- Order
- Positivity
- Relaxation
- Safety
- Space
- Trust
- Adventure
- Assurance
- Beauty
- Choice
- Compassion
- Creativity
- Encouragement
- Excitement
- Fulfillment
- Health
- Humor
- Integrity
- Joy
- Motivation
- Patience
- Pride
- Relief
- Satisfaction
- Strength
- Understanding

Although it might be easier to imagine people's 'Tough Stuff' buckets overflowing to cause outbursts or panic attacks, there can also be issues people deal with in terms of having small 'Good Stuff' buckets, for example, if they had a traumatic childhood or a very introverted personality, their buckets for Joy, Excitement and Adventure might be much smaller than you realize, so surprising them with a trip to a foreign country to go ziplining down a volcano would backfire big time because they just don't have the capacity to handle all of that. That might seem like a random scenario I just mentioned, but I'm happy to say I thoroughly enjoyed ziplining on the side of a volcano in Costa Rica with a group of friends as part of a destination wedding trip for two good friends of mine a few years back! 10 out of 10, Highly recommend! (but, of course, only if you think your buckets are up for it)

To truly round out your understanding of your unique emotional system, it's vital to acknowledge those internal obstacles that can make navigating your buckets even trickier. I call these 'Rocks.' You might also think of them as 'Blocks,' because that's precisely what they do: they're those pieces of old emotional baggage, past traumas, self-limiting beliefs, or persistent negative thoughts that not only take up valuable space in your buckets and reduce their capacity but can also act like a stubborn lid, preventing positive 'fillers' from even getting in at all. Knowing what these common 'rocks' might look like is the first step toward understanding how they impact your flow.

Here are some examples:

• Alone	• Bad	• Defective
• Different	• Guilty	• Helpless
• Hopeless	• Insignificant	• Misunderstood
• Not good enough	• Not seen	• Out of Control
• Powerless	• Stupid	• Ugly
• Unhealthy	• Unloved	• Unsafe
• Unsure	• Unwanted	• Unworthy

Now, if you found yourself nodding a lot while reading through the 'Tough Stuff' buckets or the 'Rocks' list, don't get discouraged or think, 'Oh great, I'm a lost cause!' In fact, the opposite is true. Being able to acknowledge that those things are part of your unique bucket story is actually the first and most powerful step toward making real improvements. Think about it: it's much, much easier to move a 'rock' out of your bucket when you simply know it's there!

This is where understanding how your inner world works, especially through imagery, becomes incredibly powerful. Our minds naturally respond to pictures and metaphors. Techniques like those from HeartMath (heartmath.org for more info), for example, rely heavily on imagery for transforming emotional energy. I'll talk about those techniques in more detail later in this book. The idea of emotional energy flowing into (and out of) a bucket combines beautifully with these visual tools. You can use simple imagery exercises on your own to start influencing what goes into your buckets, what comes out, and even how those 'rocks' begin to shift. Of course, if you find yourself struggling to guide yourself through those imagery techniques, ask for help!

Keep in mind, there are likely several areas of your life where you don't hesitate to ask for help. When you go to a restaurant and let someone else cook for you, that's external support. When you call a plumber or an HVAC professional to fix things in your house, that's external support. You probably don't think twice about calling these professionals because you recognize they have specialized training that you don't have, meaning they'll likely do a better job or get it fixed quicker than if you tried to do it on your own.

Well, guess what?! Handling your emotional buckets is something you probably never got actual training in either. There isn't a subject in school dedicated to teaching Emotional Intelligence (though it certainly should be on the list of things that would be far more beneficial to teach, I mean we all deal with emotions, but not everyone is gonna need Calculus in their lifetime, am I right?). If you aren't aware, Emotional Intelligence is a toolkit including a variety of techniques that help build your self-awareness and empathy towards others when it comes to emotional wellbeing and challenges in order to foster increased understanding and better communication. And while life experience might have given your parents some ability to handle their own buckets, that doesn't necessarily mean that knowledge got magically passed along to you; thankfully, you will find a variety of Emotional Intelligence techniques sprinkled throughout this book.

So, it's time to kick the stigma that you should be able to figure all this out on your own! Just like your physical capacities, your capacity to deal with your own emotions is unique, a bucket of a different size for every person. It should never be a source of comparison, embarrassment, or shame. Not being willing to reach out for help if you're struggling on your own would simply be an unfortunate failure to miss out on all the amazing improvements that are absolutely possible for you.

Chapter 2 The Essential Contents: What Fills and Nourishes Your Buckets

So, what do you do when you feel flat-out overwhelmed with stress, or you've literally had it 'up to here' with the crazy, or you're even feeling depleted and drained as if there's no hope left? Well, that's when it's time to figure out how to either drain your 'Tough Stuff' buckets if they're overflowing, or fill up your 'Good Stuff' buckets if they're feeling empty.

This reminds me of a hilarious and painfully accurate parody I've seen circulating on social media (and I love a good parody, so I must give credit where credit is due, this one is written and performed by Thomas Benjamin Wild Esq.). The lyrics go something like this: 'I've no more f#cks to give, my f#cks have runneth dry, I tried to go f#ck shopping but there's no f#cks left to buy... I've no more f#cks to give, no more f#cks I've tried to get, I'm over my f#ck budget and I'm now in f#cking debt...' If you can relate to that little ditty and desperately want to get back to giving a f#ck, this chapter is absolutely for you!

In Chapter 1, we introduced your 'Good Stuff' buckets – things like Joy, Confidence, and Connection. As you probably guessed, these buckets are designed to be filled by, well, joy, confidence, and connection! But simply knowing what they're called doesn't automatically fill them up. It's easy to run low on these essential contents, either because we're not actively seeking them out, or because we're trying to fill them with stuff that doesn't actually work long-term.

This chapter is all about understanding how to intentionally nourish these buckets, ensuring you're getting the right kind of 'fuel' to truly thrive. Unfortunately, I can't say there's a one-size-fits-all solution to filling your 'Good Stuff' buckets, but the great news is there are a lot of ways to do it, and I'm sure you'll be able to find approaches that work for you! Not only will different filling techniques work better for different people, but you might also find certain strategies are more effective depending on which specific bucket you're needing to fill. So, sit back, grab your favorite comfort snack (a bucket of popcorn maybe?), and let's dive into some bucket-filling strategies.

We've already mentioned that imagery can be an incredibly powerful tool to manage your buckets. In fact, imagery and repetition are two of the main components to a lot of powerful hypnotherapy protocols, aimed at planting new seeds of thought or establishing new neural pathways to the behaviors and responses that are healthier or more helpful for you. One of the easiest things to imagine filling a bucket with is water (or some kind of liquid). Stick with me on this... it's not difficult to imagine different colors of liquid, different densities, or even different temperatures. So, one simple strategy is to assign different colors to the types of things you want to fill your buckets. Then, close your eyes and imagine seeing that color of liquid getting poured into the appropriate bucket. That's a bit of an oversimplification, but it gives you a solid idea to start with (see Figure 3).

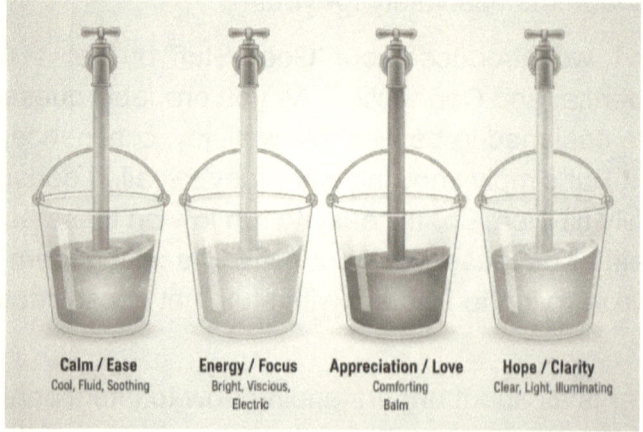

Figure 3 – Filling Buckets Imagery

Speaking of imagery, one of the most powerful and accessible techniques for influencing your emotional state comes from a practice called HeartMath. HeartMath is an organization that has done a lot of research on how our body works energetically, from a biological and scientific perspective, so even though this may seem a little 'woo-woo', trust me, it's legit! …Too legit to quit, hey, hey! (sorry, I can't help myself when words trigger song lyrics in my mind… thank you MC Hammer)

The practice is centered around something called Heart-Focused Breathing. We're not just talking about taking a few 'deep breaths'; it's about shifting your focus and intention. When you practice Heart-Focused Breathing, you're essentially guiding your system towards a state called 'coherence,' which helps calm your nervous system and makes it easier to manage your emotions. Here's how you can try it, and how it connects to those buckets:

1. **Shift Your Focus:** Gently place your attention on the area of your heart. You don't have to literally feel your heart beating, just imagine your awareness resting there. It can be helpful to close your eyes to avoid external distractions.
2. **Breathe a Little Deeper:** Now, imagine your breath flowing in and out through your heart area, as if your heart itself has lungs. Breathe a little slower and deeper than usual, and try to keep a consistent rhythm, maybe five seconds in, five seconds out. Don't strain; just find a comfortable rhythm. This helps induce the pendulum effect within your body, getting other systems in alignment so things feel like they are settling down and getting more clear.
3. **Bring in the Imagery:** As you continue to breathe as if through your heart, this is where the bucket imagery comes in! If you're working on filling your Joy Bucket, you might imagine golden, shimmering liquid flowing into your heart area with each inhale, and then radiating outwards, filling that Joy Bucket to the brim. Of course you can decide

whatever color and other qualities work best for you as your Joy Bucket filler.

4. **Sustain for a Few Minutes:** Even just a minute or two of this focused breathing can make a noticeable difference in how you feel, helping to bring a sense of balance and calm.

This simple yet profound technique gives you a direct way to interact with your emotional buckets, offering immediate relief and, with practice, increasing your capacity to handle life's various 'fills' and 'spills'. How about that? You didn't even have to read all the way to the end of the book to get to some practical, powerful strategies!! '…what can I say except "You're welcome"'. (credit to Maui from Moana for that inspiration)

So far, we've talked about filling your 'Good Stuff' buckets with things like Heart-Focused Breathing and imagery. But what about when your 'Tough Stuff' buckets are the ones sounding alarm bells, ready to spill all over the place? When you're feeling overwhelmed, agitated, or just plain done? This is where you might need to get a little creative, channeling your inner Wile E. Coyote.

Think about it: poor Wile E. spent countless hours (and his entire budget) ordering every imaginable contraption from the ACME Corporation to catch the Road Runner. (If you're not familiar with his cartoon antics from the classic Warner Bros. Looney Tunes, picture a very determined, very unlucky coyote with a penchant for elaborate, often backfiring, inventions – you can find plenty of clips online!) Most of it didn't work as planned, but he kept trying new, wild, and sometimes ridiculous inventions.

In the same way, when your Stress Bucket is about to burst, or your Anger Bucket is simmering and dangerously close to boiling over, you might need to try a few different 'ACME products' from your own personal toolkit. These aren't necessarily about filling you up; it can be just as important to actively drain or manage the overflow so you don't make a bigger mess. Maybe it's punching a punching bag, blasting some Ozzy Osbourne music (Crazy Train is a great choice… RIP Ozzy), or maybe even just screaming into a pillow. The point is, sometimes you need to get inventive with ways to prevent a full-blown emotional explosion. We'll dive into more specific strategies for draining those 'Tough Stuff' buckets later, but for now, just know that your emotional ACME catalog is vast, and finding what works for you is part of the adventure.

Just as important as knowing what fills your buckets is understanding the quality of what you're putting in. It's easy to mistake a quick fix for genuine nourishment. Think of it like trying to quench your thirst with soda instead of water. Sure, it feels good for a moment, but it doesn't truly hydrate you, and might even leave you feeling more sluggish later.

We often reach for things that offer immediate, but ultimately temporary, relief when our buckets feel low. This might look like endless scrolling on social media, overeating comfort food, or constantly seeking external validation from others. Sometimes, it can involve behaviors like smoking, drinking alcohol to numb feelings, or even relying solely on prescription medications for anxiety without addressing the root emotional causes. While some of these might offer a brief pause from discomfort, they don't actually fill the underlying emotional bucket that's craving real nourishment. In fact, many of these temporary 'fillers' can create new problems, like health issues, dependency, or a further disconnect from our true needs, essentially adding more 'rocks' to our buckets or even creating new leaks.

True, sustainable nourishment for your buckets comes from genuine sources that align with what your emotional system truly needs for long-term well-being. This is about finding authentic ways to experience joy, build genuine connection, or cultivate real peace, rather than just masking the feeling of emptiness.

Now, when it comes to understanding how our 'Good Stuff' buckets get filled, especially those related to connection, appreciation, and feeling valued, there's a brilliant framework that can shed a lot of light: The 5 Love Languages. Developed by Dr. Gary Chapman, this concept suggests that each of us has a primary way we prefer to give and receive love and appreciation. Think of these as specific 'valves' or 'receptacles' on your buckets that are uniquely designed to receive certain types of 'filler.' They can also be used to improve communication about what you need from someone else to feel better, similar to how the buckets can be used as a communication tool.

If you're trying to fill someone's Connection Bucket with, say, Words of Affirmation when their primary 'filling valve' is Acts of Service, it's like trying to fill a bucket with a leaky hose – some might get in, but a lot will be lost, and they might still feel empty. Understanding your own primary Love Language, and perhaps even those of the important people in your life, is incredibly empowering. It means you can intentionally seek out or provide the specific type of nourishment that truly makes a difference, ensuring those 'Good Stuff' buckets are getting filled in the most effective and satisfying way possible. We won't dive deep into all five here, but recognizing this concept can instantly transform how you approach nurturing your relationships and, by extension, your own emotional well-being.

The buckets we've explored so far—like Joy, Stress, Patience, and Connection—are certainly fundamental. But these are just the beginning! Your emotional bucket balancing system is incredibly nuanced, and it holds countless other specialized containers for various feelings and capacities. Think of buckets for Humor, for Abundance, for Adventure, and so many more. Just like your core buckets, these too have their unique sizes, fills, and drains, very much influencing how you experience specific aspects of life. As we continue our journey through the Emotional Bucket Balancing System, we'll dive into some of these more unique capacities, discovering how understanding them can unlock even greater self-awareness and compassion for both yourself and others.

It's crucial to understand that the practice of filling your buckets is a dynamic dance between what you do for yourself and what you receive from the world around you. There's a reason flight attendants always tell you to put on your own oxygen mask before assisting others. It's not selfish; it's practical. If your own oxygen mask isn't on and your air supply is dwindling, you'll quickly become unable to help anyone else.

The same principle applies to your emotional buckets. While external sources (relationships, validation, shared experiences) are incredibly vital, you are the primary steward of your own emotional well-being. Nobody else can be solely responsible for continually filling all your buckets. This means actively taking time for yourself, whether it's through a relaxing yoga class, a warm bath, a peaceful walk on the beach, or any activity that genuinely helps you feel rejuvenated and re-centered. If you're constantly running on empty, waiting for others to pour into you, you'll find yourself depleted, resentful, and ultimately less capable of genuinely connecting or contributing.

However, that doesn't mean it's all on you, or that you should become a hermit! We are social creatures, and many of our 'Good Stuff' buckets, like Connection, Love, and Appreciation, are designed to be filled through healthy interactions with others. The magic happens when you prioritize self-care and understand your own needs (your 'oxygen mask'), making you more resilient, more open to receiving authentic nourishment from others, and genuinely more able to give back without burning out. Knowing what truly fills you, actively pursuing it, and being open to both internal and external sources, is the key to living with consistently well-tended buckets.

"Experiencing one's self in a conscious manner—that is, gaining self-knowledge—is an integral part of learning."
- Joshua M. Freedman

Chapter 3 Strategies for Draining Your 'Tough Stuff' Buckets

In Chapter 1, we identified our unique collection of buckets, including those that hold the 'tough stuff' like stress, anger, and anxiety. Chapter 2 then explored the vital art of filling our 'Good Stuff' buckets with positive nourishment. But here's the thing: focusing only on adding good stuff, while ignoring the overflowing tough stuff, is like trying to bail out a leaky boat without patching the holes. To truly maintain your emotional equilibrium, draining your 'Tough Stuff' buckets is just as important, if not more important in moments of overwhelm, as filling your 'Good Stuff' buckets.

I'm not suggesting you'll be able to avoid discomfort entirely; but by actively processing, releasing, and reducing the emotional load so those challenging feelings don't spill over or prevent the good stuff from even finding space, you create an environment where you feel more in the flow. Think lazy river instead of white-water rapids!

When your 'Tough Stuff' buckets are brimming over with anxiety, anger, or pent-up stress, sometimes the quickest and most effective way to create some immediate space is through physical release. Think of it as opening a valve and letting the pressure out. Instead of ignoring the emotion, give that intense energy a productive outlet so it doesn't get stuck inside or explode uncontrollably.

There's a vast 'ACME catalog' of physical strategies you can try. For some, it might be the raw intensity of a long run, pushing their body until the emotional static starts to clear. For others, it's about blasting some angry music and literally shaking out the tension. A quick, contained release like screaming into a pillow can offer surprisingly immediate relief for an overflowing Anger or Frustration bucket. More structured, yet equally powerful, methods include practices like somatic yoga, which helps release trapped emotions through mindful movement and body awareness, or Tapping (Emotional Freedom Techniques - EFT), a simple yet profound method that combines light tapping on meridian points with verbalizing feelings to help process and release emotional intensity. The key is to find a movement or physical outlet that allows that trapped energy to move through you, rather than stagnating or building up.

Beyond physical release, sometimes the 'Tough Stuff' in your buckets needs a different kind of outlet: focused emotional processing. Allow yourself to explore, understand, and release those feelings, rather than just letting them sit or burst out sideways at unexpected times and inconvenient ways. One of the most accessible and potent tools for this is journaling.

The act of putting thoughts and feelings down on paper has a unique, almost magical, physical component to it. It literally helps to 'pull' the emotional energy out of your head and body, giving it a tangible form outside of you. When you're journaling to drain an overflowing bucket, the best approach is often stream-of-consciousness writing. Don't worry about spelling, grammar, punctuation, or making perfect sense. Just let the words flow. Write as if no one, not even you, will ever read it. See where your thoughts lead you, letting every frustration, fear, or sadness spill onto the page. You might be surprised at what emerges when you simply allow your mind to unload without censorship.

And to truly make it feel final, some people find it incredibly powerful to then physically destroy the paper they've written on. Tearing it up, shredding it, or even burning it (if done in a controlled, safe environment, of course!) can create a deep sense of release and finality. It's a symbolic act to 'Let it go, let it go, can't hold it back anymore' (my apologies to any parents who have heard that song from Disney's Frozen about a million times), making it feel like that emotional weight has truly left your bucket for good.

Beyond simply releasing or exploring tough emotions through journaling, we can also actively transform them. Think of it like taking the murky water from a Stress Bucket and, instead of just pouring it out, running it through a filter that changes its very composition into something clearer and more useful. This brings us to another powerful HeartMath technique known as Attitude Breathing.

Attitude Breathing builds on the Heart-Focused Breathing you learned earlier, but it adds a crucial element: intentionally activating a positive, regenerative emotion or attitude. Here's how you can practice it:

1. **Heart-Focused Breathing (Review):** Begin by shifting your attention to your heart area and breathing a little slower and deeper than usual, as if your breath is flowing in and out through your heart.

2. **Activate a Positive Attitude:** As you continue to breathe through your heart, intentionally recall or conjure up a genuine positive feeling or attitude. This could be appreciation for something in your life, care for a loved one, compassion for yourself, or an amazing sense of peace. Don't just think about it; truly feel it in your heart.

3. **Breathe the Attitude In:** Now, imagine that positive attitude or feeling flowing into your heart area with each inhale. As you exhale, imagine that positive energy radiating outward, permeating your entire being. You could even imagine it like creating a protective bubble of positive, protective energy that gets bigger and bigger until your entire body is contained within that bubble.

4. **Transforming the Tough Stuff:** The magic happens as you sustain this. If you were feeling anxious or frustrated (your Anxiety Bucket was full), hold that positive attitude. The intention is to let the gentle, coherent energy generated by the positive feeling gradually dissolve, transform the unwanted emotional energy, or even cause it to evaporate entirely, leaving more space in your bucket. It's not about fighting the negative, but about generating so much positive light that the shadows naturally recede.

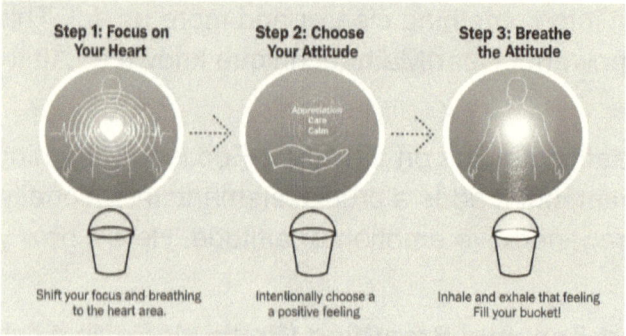

Figure 4 – HeartMath Attitude Breathing Technique

Practicing Attitude Breathing (as shown in Figure 4) for even a few minutes can create a profound shift in your emotional state, helping you move from feelings of depletion or overwhelm to a more balanced, clear, and energized state. It's like hitting a 'refresh' button for your emotional system, turning that tough stuff into something that actually gives you a boost instead of weighing you down.

Sometimes, the key to draining a 'Tough Stuff' bucket isn't about physical release or deep emotional processing of what's already there, but about changing how we perceive the 'stuff' that's trying to get in, or even what we allow to land in our buckets in the first place. This is where Mental Reframing and Perspective Shifting become incredibly powerful tools. It's about consciously choosing a different lens through which to view a situation or someone else's behavior.

One of the most essential concepts that applies here comes from Don Miguel Ruiz's The Four Agreements, specifically the agreement 'Don't Take Anything Personally.' This is a game-changer for your buckets! When someone says something rude, lashes out, or behaves in a way that feels like they're trying to dump their Anger Bucket all over you, it's so easy to absorb that and let it fill your Frustration or Hurt Bucket. But here's the secret: most of the time, their behavior isn't actually about you.

Remember how we talked about everyone having different-sized buckets, and some might already be full of 'rocks' or on the verge of overflowing? When someone snaps at you, cuts you off in traffic, or seems overly critical, it's highly likely that their Stress Bucket or Impatience Bucket is already at critical mass. You don't know what kind of day they've had, what 'rocks' they're carrying, or how close their own emotional containers are to spilling. By reminding yourself that you don't know how big or how full other people's buckets are, you can create a crucial mental buffer. Their outburst is their overflow, not a personal attack designed to fill your 'Tough Stuff' buckets. When you truly embrace 'Don't Take Anything Personally,' it creates an invisible shield, allowing their emotional 'spill' to flow right past you, leaving your buckets much lighter.

Sometimes, when a 'Tough Stuff' bucket feels like it's about to overflow, you just need a tactical timeout. You don't want to ignore your feelings forever or pretend problems don't exist; you just sometimes need a strategic distraction and diversion to create immediate mental and emotional space. Think of it as hitting a pause button on the incoming emotional deluge, giving your system a chance to reset before you figure out a more comprehensive strategy. Sometimes, you just need to channel your inner Taylor Swift and 'shake it off'!

Healthy diversions are crucial here, as opposed to unhealthy ones that might offer brief escape but add more 'rocks' in the long run, i.e., smoking, drinking alcohol, emotional eating, or other unhealthy addictive behaviors. The goal is to temporarily shift your focus to something that's genuinely engaging or calming, allowing the immediate pressure to dissipate. This could be anything from getting lost in your favorite music (especially something uplifting or soothing), diving into a captivating book or puzzle, or engaging your senses with a pleasant aroma or a mindful snack. You might take a short, brisk walk around the block, do some gentle stretching, or simply watch a light-hearted show or funny animal videos online.

The power of these diversions isn't in 'fixing' the problem, but in giving you a much-needed breather. They won't magically empty a chronically overflowing bucket, but they can definitely prevent an immediate spill. By creating that temporary mental space, you'll be better equipped to return to the tough stuff with a clearer head, more emotional capacity, and the ability to choose more intentional long-term solutions.

We've covered a lot of strategies for both proactive filling and active draining, from imagery and Attitude Breathing to physical release and mental reframing. These are powerful tools you can use daily. But let's be real: sometimes, despite your best efforts, those 'Tough Stuff' buckets just won't budge. Or maybe, you've got a few deeply embedded 'rocks' that feel impossible to move on your own. Don't think of that as a sign of weakness; it's actually a sign of wisdom to recognize when you need a little (or a lot of) help from the pros. It's also a reminder of another one of The Four Agreements, namely, 'Always do Your Best', which points out that your best can be different given different circumstances and you can never really be expected to do better than your best.

Just like you wouldn't try to perform surgery on yourself, or rewire your entire house without an electrician, your emotional system sometimes needs specialized support. Reaching out to a therapist, counselor, or a qualified coach can provide a fresh perspective, proven tools, and a safe, non-judgmental space to process what feels overwhelming. They can help you identify patterns, develop new coping mechanisms, and guide you through challenges that feel too big to tackle alone.

And when it comes to those persistent 'Rocks' (those deep-seated beliefs, past traumas, or subconscious patterns that block your capacity or prevent good stuff from getting in) one of the most effective ways to truly identify and remove them is through hypnotherapy techniques. Often, we're not even consciously aware of what these 'rocks' are, or how they got there in the first place. Hypnotherapy works with your subconscious mind, the part of you that holds onto these deeper beliefs and experiences. It's like having a skilled guide with a specialized set of tools to gently explore your inner landscape, pinpoint those hidden blocks, and facilitate their permanent release. This can lead to intense and lasting shifts, freeing up massive amounts of space in your buckets that you might not have even known was available.

An example of how things from your past can be stuck in your subconscious and affecting you without you realizing what's affecting you is demonstrated by the experience a client of mine had. He had come in wanting to address a fear of flying that seemed completely illogical to him because he had just spent his entire career as an aircraft mechanic, so he knew how safe planes were and had flown hundreds of times before with no problems. After retiring from his busy career, he started to have panic attacks when they shut the door of the aircraft. As we talked through his experience, it became apparent that it wasn't actually a fear of flying, it was claustrophobia.

When we did a regression protocol, his subconscious took him back to a time when he was young and playing with his brother in their bedroom. His brother had a book of matches and suggested they go in the closet to play with them (so they wouldn't get in trouble). Long story short, they accidentally set the house on fire… thankfully, no one was injured and the house wasn't even horribly damaged. The most interesting thing about that to me was that he didn't get punished, his parents didn't freak out, and although they were probably proud of themselves for handling it in a calm, reasonable way, recognizing it was just an accident, they had inadvertently robbed him of the opportunity to freak out about it. So, that fear got bottled up and tucked away somewhere inside until the momentum of his life slowed down to a pace (in retirement) where it could try to come back to the surface. We were able to then acknowledge those feelings and use some imagery techniques to release them, and he was able to go on his merry way.

Remember, asking for help isn't giving up; it's leveling up. Think of all the highly successful people you admire – most of them have advisors, coaches, trainers, or even personal chefs. They leverage external expertise to perform at their best. There's no shame in recognizing that some challenges benefit greatly from external expertise, especially when it comes to your emotional well-being and achieving the balance and freedom you deserve.

Chapter 4 Expanding Your Emotional Capacity: Digging Rocks Out

If you've ever felt like no matter how much 'tough stuff' you drain, or how many leaks you plug, your emotional buckets still don't feel quite as full or expansive as you'd like, you're not imagining things. Sometimes, the issue isn't what's flowing in or out, but what's permanently taking up space inside: the rocks.

Think of these rocks as deeply embedded emotional baggage, core limiting beliefs, or unresolved past experiences. Unlike the daily grit of stress or frustration, these aren't easily washed away. They sit heavy, reducing your capacity for joy, peace, and resilience, and often acting as a constant source of quiet discomfort or even outright pain. They can make you feel stuck, limit your potential, and prevent your emotional system from truly flowing freely.

In this chapter, we're going to bravely turn our attention to some of the most common and impactful 'rocks' that many of us carry. We'll explore where these heavy burdens often come from and, more importantly, begin to equip you with strategies to loosen their grip, lighten their weight, and even catapult them out of your buckets for good, expanding your emotional capacity like never before. This is where real, lasting transformation happens.

Rock 1: The "Not Good Enough" (NGE) Rock

Perhaps the most widespread and insidious 'rock' many of us carry is the deep-seated belief that we are simply 'Not Good Enough.' This is more than just occasional self-doubt; it's a pervasive internal whisper, a feeling of inadequacy that can impact every area of your life. It shows up as perfectionism, procrastination, people-pleasing, fear of failure, or an inability to truly receive compliments or acknowledge your own successes. This rock doesn't just take up space; it actively drains your Confidence, Joy, and Self-Worth Buckets, while constantly refilling your Anxiety and Shame Buckets.

Where Does This Rock Come From?
(The Sources of "Not Good Enough")

The origins of the 'Not Good Enough' rock are incredibly varied and often rooted in our formative experiences. Recognizing where it might have come from is the first step toward dislodging it:

- **Family Upbringing:** This is a primary quarry for the NGE rock. Perhaps you grew up in a household with extremely high expectations, where mistakes were heavily criticized, or where love felt conditional based on achievement. Maybe a parent or sibling frequently made comparisons, or inadvertently sent messages that you weren't smart enough, pretty enough, or strong enough. Even well-meaning parents can, through subtle cues, create the foundation for this belief if a child perceives they never quite measure up. It could even be the result of getting compared to other siblings by teachers in school.

- **Religious Background:** For some, religious teachings, particularly those focused heavily on sin, guilt, or the concept of inherent unworthiness, can contribute to the NGE rock. A strict interpretation might foster a perpetual feeling that no matter what you do, you're falling short of divine expectations or moral perfection.

- **Societal Views and Conditioning:** Society itself is a powerful sculptor of our beliefs about 'enoughness.' These messages are often subtle but pervasive:
  - **Race:** Systemic racism and cultural biases can instill feelings of inadequacy or being 'less than' based on racial

identity, impacting opportunities, self-perception, and a sense of belonging.

o **Gender:** Traditional gender roles or societal expectations about how men and women should behave, look, or achieve can lead to feelings of not being feminine/masculine enough, not fitting norms, or facing limitations based on gender.

o **Social Class & Financial Position:** Messages about success often equate worth with wealth or social status. Growing up in poverty, or experiencing financial instability, can deeply implant the belief that one isn't 'good enough' to achieve financial security or social standing, leading to feelings of shame or inadequacy compared to perceived societal ideals.

o **Other Factors:** Beyond these, societal pressures related to physical appearance, academic achievement, career success, relationship status, or even social media's highlight reels can constantly broadcast a message that everyone else is doing better, achieving more, or simply is more, reinforcing the NGE rock within.

Acknowledging that these are external influences, not inherent truths about your worth, is the beginning of reclaiming your emotional space. This rock isn't who you are; it's something you've unknowingly picked up along the way. Now, let's look at how we can start to dislodge it and catapult it out of your bucket.

Understanding where your 'Not Good Enough' rock comes from is a crucial first step, but the real breakthrough comes in actively dislodging it. You're not going to magically erase a deeply ingrained belief overnight; but with persistent, compassionate work to loosen its grip, eventually you can catapult it out of your bucket, freeing up immense emotional capacity.

Catapulting the 'Not Good Enough' Rock Out of Your Bucket (Strategies for Reclaiming Your Worth)

The process of removing the NGE rock involves a shift in awareness, a cultivation of self-compassion, and a willingness to take action that defies the old narrative, or as Kelly Clarkson might say... 'What doesn't kill you makes you stronger, stand a little taller...'.

1. **Identify and Interrogate the Voice:**
   o **Listen Closely:** The NGE rock often manifests as a critical inner voice. Become keenly aware of when it speaks: 'You're going to mess this up,' 'Why even try?,' 'You're not smart enough for this,' 'Everyone else is better.' If you have a hard time identifying it yourself, ask a trusted friend or family member to help point it out. It can be easier to see if from the outside than from the inside sometimes.
   o **Question Its Authority:** Once you hear it, don't automatically believe it. Ask yourself:
      ▪ Is this thought a fact or a belief? (Often, it's just a belief.)
      ▪ Whose voice is this, really? (Is it an echo of a parent, a teacher, a past bully, or a societal message?)
      ▪ What's the evidence FOR this belief? What's the evidence AGAINST it? (You'll often find a mountain of evidence against it, once you start looking for it.)
      ▪ Is this thought serving me, or holding me back?
   o **Separate Self from Story:** Recognize that the NGE narrative is a story you've absorbed, not your inherent truth. You are not your thoughts; you are the one observing them.

2. **Cultivate Radical Self-Compassion:**
   o **Be Your Own Best Friend:** If a dear friend came to you with the same self-critical thoughts, would you agree with them? Of course not! You'd offer kindness, understanding, and reassurance. Turn that same boundless compassion inward.

- o **Acknowledge the Pain:** The NGE rock often comes from pain. That pain can often be measured by the gap between our expectations and reality. Acknowledge that the younger you absorbed this belief as a form of protection or survival. Thank that part of you for trying to keep you safe, and then gently let it know it's no longer serving you.
- o **Self-Nurturing Affirmations (with feeling):** Beyond just repeating positive phrases, truly feel them. Close your eyes (or look at yourself in the mirror), place a hand over your heart, and feel the truth of statements like: 'I am enough,' 'I am worthy of love and belonging just as I am,' 'My worth is inherent, not earned.' While this may seem awkward at first, this is about cultivating a new emotional truth. Repetition combined with the emotional energy of positive feelings about the change you're wanting to see makes it even more enticing to the subconscious to pay attention to. Additionally, engaging as many senses as you can to reinforce these affirmations can also be helpful. I like to say "Write it, See it, Say it, Hear it" which reminds me of that song by Daft Punk, "Harder, Better, Faster, Stronger." And believe it or not, using these techniques can make you stronger.

3. **Take Imperfect Action:**
   - o **Defy the Narrative:** The NGE rock thrives on inaction and playing it safe. The most powerful way to dislodge it is to take small, consistent steps despite the fear or doubt it creates. Don't wait until you feel good enough; take action to become good enough through experience.
   - o **Embrace 'Good Enough' over 'Perfect':** Perfectionism is a common byproduct of NGE. Instead of aiming for flawless, aim for completion, for learning, for progress.
   - o **Celebrate Every Micro-Victory:** Remember our discussion about celebrating small wins? Every time you push past the NGE whisper and take action, even a tiny one, you're filling

your Confidence Bucket and eroding the NGE rock. Acknowledge it!

4. **Reframe Mistakes as Data, Not Verdicts:**
    o **Mistakes, setbacks, or 'failures'** are often interpreted by the NGE rock as definitive proof of its validity. Challenge this. Remember that before this rock settled in, you didn't give up on trying to walk just because you fell a few times as a toddler while trying to learn.
    o **Learning Opportunities:** Reframe them as valuable data points, opportunities to learn and adjust, or simply an inevitable part of being human and trying new things. Did it really prove you're not good enough, or just that a particular approach didn't work this time?

5. **The Subconscious Shift: A Deeper Dive with Hypnotherapy:**
    o **While these conscious strategies are powerful,** the NGE rock is often deeply embedded in your subconscious mind, having been laid down and built upon over years. This is where tools like hypnotherapy can be uniquely transformative. By accessing the subconscious through a relaxed, focused state, you can directly challenge and reframe these old limiting beliefs at their root, installing new, empowering narratives that genuinely support your inherent worth. It's like using dynamite to explode the rock into small bits, rather than just chipping away at the surface.

Dismantling the 'Not Good Enough' rock is an insightful act of self-liberation. It frees up immense emotional real estate in your buckets, allowing you to fill them with genuine confidence, joy, and a powerful sense of self-worth that is truly yours, unburdened by old, outdated stories.

Rock 2: The "Fears" Rock
While the 'Not Good Enough' rock often whispers about your inherent worth, the 'Fears' rock is more about perceived threats and potential dangers. This rock is a deep-seated apprehension

that, when allowed to sit in your bucket, can paralyze you, restrict your movement, drain your Energy and Courage Buckets, and prevent new, positive experiences from flowing in. It often manifests as chronic worry, phobias, social anxiety, performance anxiety, or a general reluctance to step outside your comfort zone.

Where Does This Rock Come From? The Roots of Your Fears
Fears, like the NGE rock, often have a history. They aren't random; they're usually learned or developed in response to specific experiences or teachings:

- **Past Negative Experiences (Direct Trauma/Pain):** If you've had a genuinely negative or traumatic experience (e.g., public speaking disaster, a painful breakup, a financial loss, a physical injury), your brain creates a strong association between that situation and potential pain. This can lead to a fear-rock that proclaims, "Don't go there again!" to protect you.
- **Learned Fears (Observational Learning):** We often inherit fears without ever having a direct negative experience ourselves. This might come from:
  - **Parental Warnings:** Overprotective parents or those with their own anxieties might inadvertently instill fears in us about the world, strangers, specific activities, or even emotions. It's not uncommon for many parents to be more protective of first-born or only children, so even your birth order can have an effect on your bucket system.
  - **Societal Narratives:** News, social media, and cultural stories can amplify fears about safety, health, success, or social acceptance, making us apprehensive about everyday situations.
- **Anticipation of Future Pain/Discomfort:** Sometimes, fear isn't about what has happened, but what might happen. This rock is built from projecting negative outcomes into the future – the fear of failure, rejection, embarrassment, or even success itself. It's the mind trying to protect you from hypothetical hurt.

- **Loss of Control & The Unknown:** A significant source of fear is the feeling of lacking control. This rock often grows when we face situations where the outcome is uncertain or outside our influence. The unknown, by its very nature, can be terrifying to a mind that craves predictability and safety.

Understanding these origins helps depersonalize the fear. It's not a flaw in you; it's a protective mechanism that has become overactive and is now hindering, rather than helping, your flow and keeping you stuck in place.

Catapulting the 'Fears' Rock Out of Your Bucket: Strategies for Cultivating Courage

Confronting fear requires a blend of gentle self-awareness and courageous, incremental action. The goal isn't to eliminate fear entirely – a healthy dose of caution is useful – but to ensure it doesn't become a rock that paralyzes your progress and drains your joy.

1. **Acknowledge and Name It:** The first step is to bring the fear out of the shadows. When you feel that tightness in your chest, that racing thought, that urge to retreat, pause and ask: 'What exactly am I afraid of right now?' Naming the specific fear reduces its amorphous power. So get as specific as possible in figuring out what the basic, fundamental thing is that you are truly afraid of.

2. **Distinguish Real Danger from Perceived Danger:** Your brain's alarm system (the amygdala) often can't tell the difference between a tiger in the room and a perceived social threat. Ask yourself: 'Is this a life-or-death situation, or is my brain just trying to protect me from discomfort or perceived embarrassment?' Most fears we face daily fall into the latter category, and we can turn down the intensity of our reaction.

3. **Take Micro-Steps into the Discomfort (Exposure):** One of the ways to truly shrink a fear rock is to gradually expose yourself to what you fear, in small, manageable doses. If you fear public speaking, start by speaking up in a small meeting,

then offer to lead a short presentation, then a slightly longer one. Each successful micro-step fills your Courage Bucket and chips away at the fear rock.

4. **Focus on What You Can Control:** Fear often thrives on what's outside our control. Shift your focus and energy to what you can control: your preparation, your effort, your response, your breathing. Letting go of the illusion of control over outcomes can absolutely lighten the fear burden. You might also remind yourself of similar situations you managed to survive or conquer in the past, to reinforce a sense that you have been here before, so it's not completely unknown.

5. **Mental Rehearsal and Visualization:** Before facing a feared situation, mentally walk through it in a positive way. Visualize yourself successfully navigating it, feeling confident and calm. Our brains often can't distinguish between vividly imagined experience and real experience, building neural pathways for success. This can be boosted even more with a custom hypnotic recording.

6. **Utilize Your Breath (HeartMath Connection):** When fear takes hold, your nervous system often goes into fight-or-flight. Conscious breathing, like the Heart-Focused Breathing we discussed earlier, can quickly calm your nervous system, signaling safety to your brain and preventing the fear from escalating into panic.

7. **Embrace Faith as an Antidote:** For many, cultivating faith can be a profound counterweight to fear. Whether it's faith in a higher power, faith in the universe's benevolent design, or simply faith in your own resilience and ability to overcome, this deep trust can dissolve the apprehension that is found in some Fear Rocks. Faith doesn't mean the absence of challenges, but the unwavering belief that you possess the inner resources or external support to meet them. It shifts your focus from perceived threats to underlying stability and purpose, acting as a powerful balm for a worried mind.

8. **Seek Professional Support:** For intense fears, phobias, or anxieties that deeply impact your life, professional support (therapy, hypnotherapy) can be invaluable. These modalities can help you gently reprocess past experiences and reprogram subconscious responses to fear, effectively dissolving the rock at its core.

Confronting your fears is an important act of self-love. It expands your world, allowing new experiences and opportunities to flow into your life that were previously blocked by the heavy weight of apprehension.

Rock 3: The "Shame" Rock

Okay, so let's talk about the 'Shame' rock. Now, don't confuse this with a 'shamrock' – a lovely, lucky green clover! While 'shame rock' might sound a bit like its leafy cousin, there's absolutely nothing lucky or light about carrying this particular burden. This is a heavy, isolating weight that often convinces you that you are fundamentally flawed, unworthy of connection, or inherently bad due to something you've done, experienced, or even just are. Shame thrives in secrecy, compelling us to hide parts of ourselves, leading to weighty emotional isolation and taking up massive space in our Connection, Self-Acceptance, and Joy Buckets. It's the gut-wrenching feeling that if others truly knew the real you, they would reject you outright.

Where Does This Rock Come From? The Roots of Shame

Shame, unlike guilt (which is about doing something bad), is about being bad. It also goes a step or two beyond just not being good enough. Its origins are often deeply interpersonal and tied to early experiences of judgment or rejection:

- **Early Childhood Experiences:** This is a primary breeding ground for shame. If a child is consistently shamed for expressing emotions, making mistakes, or simply being themselves, they internalize the message that something about them is fundamentally wrong or unlovable. This can come from harsh criticism, humiliation, neglect, or abuse.

- **Family Secrets & Dysfunctional Dynamics:** Families with unspoken rules, secrets, or a culture of blame can inadvertently foster shame. Children may feel responsible for protecting the family image, leading to a hidden sense of being tainted or wrong.
- **Societal and Cultural Stigmas:** Society places judgments on many aspects of identity and experience. Being part of a marginalized group (based on race, gender, sexual orientation, disability, mental health struggles, socioeconomic status, etc.) can lead to internalized shame due to societal prejudice or discrimination. Similarly, societal expectations around success, body image, or conventional life paths can make individuals feel inherently shameful if they don't conform.
- **Religious Conditioning:** As with the NGE rock, certain religious doctrines, particularly those emphasizing moral failings, sin, and eternal damnation, can instill deep-seated shame for natural human desires, thoughts, or actions, leading to a pervasive feeling of being inherently unworthy.
- **Traumatic Experiences:** Experiencing trauma, particularly interpersonal trauma, can leave survivors with intense shame, often believing it was their fault, or that they are now somehow 'damaged' or 'dirty.' This can be seen in some children of divorce, especially if they've ever seen their parents arguing about something related to them. Their minds can create a connection that ties them to the decision to split up even if it's not actually there.

Shame often makes us want to disappear, to isolate, and to keep our 'bad' parts hidden. But like all rocks, its power lies in its hidden nature. Bringing it into the light is the first step to dissolving it.

Catapulting the 'Shame' Rock Out of Your Bucket: Strategies for Cultivating Self-Acceptance

Removing the shame rock is perhaps the most delicate, yet ultimately freeing, process. It requires courage, vulnerability, and a profound commitment to self-compassion.

1. **Bring It into the Light (Speak Your Story):** Shame thrives in secrecy. The most powerful antidote to shame is often connection and vulnerability. Find a safe, trusted person (a therapist, a close friend, a supportive family member) and share the story of your shame. Speaking it out loud, and having it met with empathy and acceptance, is incredibly healing. You'll likely discover that your 'shameful' experience is a common human one, reducing its isolating power.

2. **Separate Self from Behavior:** Remember the core difference: guilt is about what you did, shame is about who you are. Challenge the narrative that a mistake or an experience defines your entire worth. You might have done something you regret, but that does not make you an inherently bad or unworthy person. Focus on the behavior, learn from it, and let go of the judgment of your inherent being. This is an incredibly helpful and important distinction, worthy of repeating to yourself until it feels obvious.

3. **Practice Self-Compassion (Unconditionally):** This is where radical self-acceptance comes in. Treat yourself with the same unconditional kindness and understanding you would offer a beloved child or a friend going through a difficult time. Acknowledge your pain, offer yourself comfort, and validate your humanity, flaws and all. If this is difficult for you at first and you don't have supportive family or friends, seek out a good therapist.

4. **Challenge the Inner Critic:** The shame rock is often fueled by a harsh inner critic. Just as with the NGE rock, listen to this voice and question its validity. Is it truly helping you, or just keeping you trapped in a cycle of self-condemnation? Replace its harsh judgments with kinder, more understanding self-talk.

5. **Reclaim Your Narrative:** Shame often comes from a story we've been told about ourselves, or a story we've created based on painful experiences. You have the power to rewrite that narrative. Focus on your resilience, your lessons learned,

and your inherent worth. Your past experiences don't have to define your future.

6. **Seek Professional Guidance (Crucial for Deep Shame):** For deeply ingrained shame, especially that stemming from trauma or chronic invalidation, professional guidance from a therapist or hypnotherapist is highly recommended (or if you happen to have a leprechaun in your pocket... no wait, it's NOT a shamrock, never mind). These professionals can provide a safe space and specific techniques to help you gently reprocess past experiences, release stored emotional pain, and reprogram subconscious beliefs about your worth and identity.

Releasing the shame rock is a journey toward thoughtful self-acceptance and authentic connection. It allows you to step fully into your true self, unburdened by the weight of judgment, and open your buckets to the deep wellsprings of joy, peace, and belonging.

Beyond the general feelings of Shame, Fear, or 'Not Good Enough,' some 'rocks' manifest as specific limitations, like a stunted Abundance Bucket or a restricted sense of feeling Deserving. For instance, if you grew up in a family where money was consistently tight, or where the message was that 'we don't have enough,' you might unknowingly carry a very small, constricted Abundance Bucket. This can show up in so many ways for so many people, we all probably have something from our past that continues to have a similar influence over us, so there's no use in placing blame or sulking in it. The power comes in recognizing that this historical conditioning can limit your current capacity to receive prosperity or feel truly worthy of good things – whether that's financial wealth, fulfilling relationships, or even simple joys.

But here's the empowering truth: the size of your Abundance or Deserving Bucket is not set in stone. Just like any other capacity, you can, through conscious effort, expand it. This involves activities like spending more time around people who comfortably embody a larger Abundance Bucket, allowing yourself to feel more at ease with prosperity; engaging in vision boarding and dreaming big without self-judgment; or actively asking for mentorship and guidance from those who have successfully expanded their own capacity for abundance.

This brings us to a crucial point about all these 'rocks' and smaller buckets: you don't have to fix them alone. We wouldn't hesitate to call a plumber to fix a leak in our house, or an electrician for a wiring issue. And I assure you, the people who demonstrate vast Abundance in their lives are NOT doing everything themselves – they hire people to take care of their security, clean their home, cook their food, manage their investments, and so much more. Since we don't even get basic training in emotional bucket balancing in school, we most certainly aren't natural-born bucket experts, just like we aren't naturally-born plumbers or financial advisors. Recognizing when you need help, and actively seeking support from coaches, therapists, or mentors who have expanded their own 'buckets' in areas where you feel limited, is one of the most powerful ways to truly expand your emotional capacity.

Chapter 5 Optimizing Your Bucket System: Plugging Leaks and Enhancing Flow

So far, we've focused on getting your buckets straight: understanding what they hold, how to fill your 'Good Stuff' buckets, how to strategically drain those overflowing 'Tough Stuff' buckets, and strategies to remove some common Rocks. In order to master your emotional bucket balancing system, you need to be able to manage crises when they hit as well as being proactive in supporting your long-term mental health. Think of it like this: you wouldn't just fix a burst pipe in your house; you'd also want to seal up any slow, hidden leaks that are constantly dripping away your valuable resources. This chapter is all about moving beyond immediate fixes to truly optimizing your emotional buckets, ensuring they're not just managed, but thriving, and ready to handle whatever life throws your way.

You know that annoying drip under the sink that you keep meaning to fix, but it's not a burst pipe, so you let it go? And then suddenly, there's a damp spot on the floor, and you realize how much water has actually been wasted over time? That's exactly what 'leaks' are in your emotional bucket balancing system. These aren't the sudden overflows we talked about in Chapter 3, but rather subtle, often unnoticed drains that slowly siphon off your valuable good stuff or continuously feed into your 'Tough Stuff' buckets, making it feel like you're constantly refilling without ever getting ahead.

These leaks can manifest in many forms. They might look like procrastination, constantly putting off important tasks that then become a heavy Stress Bucket burden. Perhaps it's perfectionism, draining your Joy Bucket because nothing ever feels 'good enough.' Unhealthy boundaries or people-pleasing are massive leaks, allowing others' demands and expectations to drain your Energy or Peace Buckets. Constant self-criticism slowly erodes your Confidence and Self-Esteem Buckets. Even neglecting basic needs like adequate sleep, nutrition, or movement can be silent leaks, steadily depleting your Energy Bucket and making all other tough stuff feel heavier. Taking on too much, saying 'yes' when you mean 'no,' or dwelling on past regrets are also common culprits that can leave you feeling perpetually drained.

The insidious nature of leaks is that they're often so habitual, so much a part of our daily patterns, that we don't even recognize them as drains until our buckets are dangerously low. It's like trying to fill a bathtub with the drain plug out – no matter how much good stuff you pour in, it just keeps seeping away.

So, how do you actually spot these sneaky leaks in your own bucket system? They're often so subtle that you might not notice them until your Energy Bucket feels completely empty, or your Patience Bucket has dwindled to nothing for no apparent reason. One of the most telling signs that you might have a leak (or several!) is a consistent feeling of being drained.

Figure 5 – Patience Bucket Leaks Causing Overreaction

This can show up in more ways than physical tiredness (see Figure 5); it's an emotional and mental fatigue that persists even after rest. Think about your day-to-day activities, interactions, and even your thought patterns. Which ones consistently leave you feeling zapped, irritable, or deflated? Does a specific conversation always make your Joy Bucket feel a little emptier? Does endless scrolling on social media, which might start as a distraction, actually leave your Energy Bucket lower than before? Do certain commitments, even ones you 'should' do, leave you feeling utterly spent? These persistent energy drains are often direct indicators that a leak is siphoning off your valuable emotional resources.

Sometimes, these drains are directly connected to our unmet needs for connection and appreciation. Remember The 5 Love Languages we discussed in Chapter 2? If your primary Love Language is Words of Affirmation, and you're surrounded by people who rarely offer verbal praise or encouragement, that lack isn't just a missed opportunity to fill your Confidence Bucket; it can actually act as a slow leak, steadily draining your sense of worthiness or motivation. Similarly, if Acts of Service is your language and you're constantly doing everything for everyone else without receiving help in return, your Energy Bucket will quickly run dry, leaving you feeling unsupported and depleted. Paying attention to these unmet 'Love Language' needs can reveal significant leaks in your system.

Beyond just noticing a feeling of being drained, another important way to identify your leaks is through mindfulness. You've probably heard the word 'mindfulness' tossed around a lot, but at its heart, it's pretty simple: it's the practice of paying attention to the present moment, on purpose, and without judgment. It's about truly noticing what's happening inside you and around you, right now, rather than getting swept away by thoughts about the past or worries about the future.

You don't need to sit cross-legged on a mountaintop to be mindful. You can practice it pretty much anywhere, anytime. It might be taking a moment to truly feel your breath, noticing the sensations in your body as you walk, or even fully engaging your senses while drinking a cup of coffee. The 'how' is simply slowing down enough to observe, without immediately trying to change or fix anything. It can be more difficult to do in a loud environment or with your eyes open when there's lots of visual stimulation, so if possible, try to find a moment to step away and focus inward, just for a few moments. Thankfully, it doesn't have to turn into full-fledged meditation to be helpful. I mean, I'm a hypnotherapist and I've led guided meditations for years, but I still struggle to 'empty my mind' like a lot of meditation die-hards suggest.

How does this apply to your leaks? Well, those leaks, by their nature, are often subtle drips. If you're constantly rushing through life, distracted by a million things, you're unlikely to notice the slow seep of your Joy Bucket or the persistent drip into your Stress Bucket. Keeping in mind, from Ruiz' The Four Agreements, the agreement 'Be Impeccable With Your Word', when you say what you mean and mean what you say, you're less likely to have to worry about being called out on inconsistencies or causing more confusion, which could eventually drain your Confidence or Integrity Buckets.

Mindfulness helps you become the diligent plumber of your own emotional system. By simply observing, you start to see patterns: 'Every time I have this particular conversation, my Patience Bucket feels empty,' or 'After spending an hour on that social media app, my Confidence Bucket feels significantly lighter.' You begin to spot those recurring situations, thoughts, or interactions that consistently lead to a specific emotional drain or fill. This heightened awareness gives you the critical information you need to pinpoint exactly where those leaks are, and therefore, where you need to focus your efforts.

In addition to noticing energy drains and practicing mindfulness, another powerful way to pinpoint your leaks is through direct self-reflection. The good news is, just by reading this book and becoming aware of the 'bucket' metaphor, you've already started to fine-tune your internal radar! This newfound awareness should make it easier to pause, observe what's happening with your emotions, and actively seek out strategies to bring back balance.

To guide your self-reflection, try asking yourself questions that encourage honest, in-the-moment observation. Think of it as an exercise in curiosity, not judgment:

- 'After that interaction, do I feel more encouraged or more discouraged?'
- 'Am I forcing a smile, or does it feel authentic, like I'm happy from the inside out?'
- 'Which of my emotions was at the control panel driving my reaction?' (If you're familiar with the Inside Out movies, you'll know exactly what we're talking about here – was it Joy, Sadness, Anger, Fear, or maybe even Anxiety or Envy taking the lead?)
- 'When did my Energy Bucket start feeling low today?'
- 'What thought or situation consistently makes my Patience Bucket feel like it's shrinking?'

Sometimes, despite our best efforts at self-reflection, our leaks can be in our blind spots. We're so used to certain patterns that we don't even see them as issues. This is where a trusted friend or family member can be incredibly helpful. Choose someone you know is honest, caring, and can offer a perspective without judgment. You might ask them, 'Hey, have you ever noticed if [specific situation/person] seems to consistently leave me feeling [drained/irritable]?' or 'Do you ever see me do [specific behavior] that seems to zap my energy?' Their external observation, combined with your growing self-awareness, can illuminate leaks you never knew were there, giving you crucial information for plugging them up. If you don't feel like you have a non-judgmental friend or family member who can offer this kind of support, this is another great use of a therapist, hypnotherapist, or life coach –

they are trained to help you uncover these blind spots and navigate them effectively.

Identifying your leaks is a huge victory, but the real magic happens when you start plugging them up. This is where awareness transforms into intentional action. And just like fixing that dripping faucet, the first step is often to write things down. Get specific about the leak you've identified and then brainstorm a plan for how you intend to address it. Putting it on paper makes it real, tangible, and much harder to ignore. It's your personal repair manual for your emotional buckets.

Once you have a plan, even a small one, consider sharing it with someone who can help keep you accountable. This isn't about shame or judgment; it's about inviting a trusted person into your journey to offer encouragement and gentle reminders. Sometimes, just knowing someone else is rooting for your bucket's health can make all the difference.

Let's take a common leak: being drained by certain people. If you've identified that spending time with a particular individual consistently siphons off your Energy Bucket or fills your Frustration Bucket, your plan might involve setting a clear boundary. You could promise yourself that you will only spend a certain, limited amount of time around them, or schedule your interactions strategically to protect your energy. And remember those imagery techniques we've talked about? You could visualize their words or negativity floating by you like leaves on a lazy river, instead of sticking to you like velcro. This allows you to mentally deflect their 'spill' without absorbing it.

I remember having a client, shortly after starting my hypnotherapy practice, who was deeply embedded in victim mentality. Any time I mentioned a possible path to improvement, she had a reason it wouldn't work for her. I let her go on longer than I should have at first, but I started to notice that I was having headaches after her sessions, and that didn't happen for my other clients. So I had to get more proactive in stopping her from deflecting my questions with long explanations about why it wasn't her fault and stories about all the struggles she faced in her life. Her Self Esteem Bucket was almost entirely depleted, and it was sucking the life out of my buckets of Hope and Patience. And guess what, by establishing better boundaries, she stopped droning on about how hopeless her situation was… and my headaches went away (I'm trying hard to NOT hear the N'Sync lyrics to "Bye Bye Bye" in my head right now, but it's not working).

The key is to decide on whatever action makes sense to stop that specific leak. Whether it's practicing saying 'no' more often, scheduling dedicated 'me-time' to counter a depletion, setting stricter limits on social media, or consciously reframing self-critical thoughts, every action counts. Write it down so you can remind yourself and hold yourself accountable to it. And here's the crucial part: do this without harsh judgment. Acknowledge even small amounts of progress, celebrate the attempts, and if you slip up, simply encourage yourself to keep trying. The goal is progress, not perfection, in keeping your emotional buckets full and happy.

Now that we've explored identifying and plugging the more obvious leaks, let's talk about a more subtle, yet incredibly pervasive, way your energy can drain away. This brings us to a profound concept from Gay Hendricks' brilliant book, The Big Leap. Hendricks introduces the idea that we each operate in different 'Zones' of our abilities, and understanding these zones is key to maximizing our sense of fulfillment and, you guessed it, keeping your emotional buckets brimming.

He identifies four zones:

- **The 'Zone of Incompetence':** This is pretty straightforward. These are tasks you're just plain bad at, or that you dislike intensely. Doing anything here is a massive energy drain and fills your Frustration or Stress  Bucket instantly. Think trying to fix your own car engine when you know nothing about mechanics, or doing your own complex taxes when numbers make your head spin. It's definitely an area to delegate whenever possible!

- **The 'Zone of Competence':** These are tasks you can do, but  others can do them just as well, if not better. You're competent, but it doesn't light you up. This is where many of us spend too much time, doing things that are 'fine' but don't energize us. It's not necessarily a 'Tough Stuff' bucket filler, but it can be a slow leak on your Energy or Joy Bucket.

- **The 'Zone of Excellence':** This is where you excel. You're really, really good at these things. People praise you for them, and you might even enjoy them. Many of us build successful careers and lives operating mostly in our 'Zone of Excellence', and it feels great to be recognized for our skills! However,

even operating in your 'Zone of Excellence', while highly rewarding, isn't always fully regenerative for your deepest energy reserves. You might be good at it, but if it doesn't align with your most authentic passions and unique gifts, it can subtly prevent your Joy or  Authenticity Buckets from reaching their fullest, most effortless capacity. For example, I was a thriving human factors engineer, making a six-figure income. From the outside, I was successful. But I didn't feel like I was making as big a difference as I was capable of making in the world or for people. Through a variety of things falling into place, I decided to leave that career and open my own hypnotherapy practice. While the salary didn't quite match, I am POSITIVE that I now make MUCH bigger impacts on many people's lives, which gives me a much bigger sense of fulfillment. Staying in your 'Zone of Excellence' is not a 'leak' in the sense of being bad, but rather a missed opportunity to tap into something even more sustaining.

- **The 'Zone of Genius':** This is the sweet spot. These are the activities where your unique talents and passions intersect. Time seems to disappear when you're in this zone. It feels effortless, joyful, and completely authentic. You're doing something that only you can do in your unique way, and it  actually fills your Energy and Fulfillment Buckets simply by doing it. As a hypnotherapist, I've had many times when I've spent more than three hours with a new client, getting to know as much as I can about them to provide the best experience or transformation. That time just flies by! I don't even realize when I've worked all day with clients and missed a meal because it feels so good and energizing. Keep in mind, this doesn't need to be linked to a career change, you can find ways to work in activities that are in your 'Zone of Genius' as a hobby, a side hustle, or just a volunteer activity you can enjoy from time to time to help fill your 'Good Stuff' buckets.

The subtle 'leak' for most people often comes from spending too much time in their 'Zone of Competence or Excellence'. While they might be good at these things, they aren't always deeply energizing or uniquely you. Every hour spent doing something in your 'Zone of Competence or Excellence' that isn't your unique genius, is an hour not spent doing what truly brings you alive and effortlessly refills your most important buckets!

This framework is incredibly helpful for understanding what you can truly handle on your own versus what it's better to ask someone else to help with. If a task consistently pulls you into your 'Zone of Incompetence' or heavily drains you in your 'Zone of

Competence', that's a glaring leak. It's an invitation to delegate, automate, or seek external support (remember those therapists, coaches, and even personal chefs we talked about!). By consciously shifting more of your time and energy into your 'Zone of Genius', you're not just plugging leaks, you're literally enhancing the flow of positive energy into your entire bucket system, allowing your unique gifts to truly shine and sustain you.

As we close out this chapter, take a moment to appreciate the powerful shift you've begun. You've moved beyond just reacting to overflowing 'Tough Stuff' buckets and are now actively becoming the master of your entire emotional bucket balancing system! We've uncovered how 'leaks' – those subtle, often unnoticed drains like procrastination, people-pleasing, or operating outside your true gifts – can quietly deplete your valuable good stuff or allow unwanted tough stuff to seep in.

You've learned practical ways to spot these leaks: by tuning into consistent energy drains (including unmet Love Language needs), practicing mindful observation of recurring patterns, asking insightful self-reflection questions, and even seeking the honest perspective of trusted friends or professionals. And most importantly, you now have concrete strategies for plugging those leaks, from writing down action plans and leveraging accountability, to using powerful imagery and understanding the intense impact of working in your 'Zone of Genius' (and knowing when to delegate from your 'Zones of Competence or Incompetence').

This chapter marks a significant step towards long-term emotional health. You're moving beyond bailing out the boat; you're patching the holes and ensuring your vessel is built for smooth sailing. The insights here empower you to proactively preserve your precious emotional resources and continually enhance your capacity for joy and fulfillment.

But here's the thing: we don't live in a bubble. Our buckets are constantly interacting with the buckets of others. Sometimes, someone else's overflowing 'Tough Stuff' bucket can splash onto us, or our own judgments about their perceived 'fullness' can actually weigh us down. In Chapter 6: Others' Buckets: Compassion, Connection, and Releasing Judgment, we'll explore how applying the bucket metaphor to the people around you can dramatically reduce your own stress, foster deeper understanding, and truly revolutionize your relationships.

"You can't control how someone else feels, but you can control how you show up."
- Jay Shetty

Chapter 6 Others' Buckets: Compassion, Connection, and Releasing Judgment

By now, you're becoming a bona fide expert on your own emotional buckets. You know what fills them, what drains them, how to spot those sneaky leaks, and even how to make them hum with the energy of your 'Zone of Genius'. But here's the often-overlooked truth: we don't exist in a vacuum. Every single day, your emotional buckets are interacting with the emotional buckets of everyone around you – your family, friends, co-workers, and even the stranger who cuts you off in traffic.

It's incredibly easy, and completely human, to focus solely on our own internal experience. When someone lashes out, ignores us, or seems grumpy, our first instinct is often to take it personally. Our own Hurt or Anger Bucket might immediately start filling up. But what if you could dramatically reduce the impact of others' tough stuff on your own system? What if understanding their invisible buckets could be the key to unlocking more peace, compassion, and less judgment in your life? This has been the driving force for me through most of my life, trying to help people get along with each other and be happier with themselves. I even named my business EPIC Renewal back in 2014 with EPIC being an acronym for External Peace, Internal Calm.

The core insight here is simple yet significant: people's actions are almost always a reflection of their bucket levels, not a personal attack on you. This is where two of those brilliant agreements from The Four Agreements come into play, with an even deeper layer of understanding: 'Don't Make Assumptions' and 'Don't Take Anything Personally'. When someone is irritable, it's rarely because you, specifically, are annoying them (unless you just emptied a bucket full of their personal pet peeves on them, in which case, fair play!). More often, their Patience Bucket is bone dry, their Stress Bucket is overflowing, or their Anxiety Bucket is filled with sharp, jagged rocks. Their external behavior is simply the overflow or the desperate cry of their internal system. It's not about you, even if it's directed at you.

I've learned this lesson firsthand several times. I remember one time, a friend I'd known and played volleyball with for many years started complaining intensely that I wasn't setting him enough in our league game, and that everyone knew where I was going to set the ball. This seemed completely out of the blue to me, especially since I was actually known in our league for being deceptive with my set choices, often confusing blockers on the other side of the net! His accusations at first poured straight into my Confusion Bucket, and as he kept pushing, it quickly spilled into my Anger and Frustration Buckets. Only because I'm not a very confrontational person did it not explode into a huge argument right then and there.

It took me a while to process it, but then I remembered he had told me his girlfriend broke up with him unexpectedly just a few days before. She wasn't responding to him, so he couldn't direct his pain at her. And there I was, available, so he was unconsciously spilling those buckets of Hurt, Disappointment, and Resentment in my direction. Once I recognized that underlying truth, my own Anger dissipated almost instantly. I felt no need to confront him about the volleyball sets anymore, because I knew my set selection in a random league game was truly not that important in the grand scheme of things. Understanding his buckets saved my buckets from a lot of unnecessary tough stuff. And notice, I didn't have to get physical evidence or proof that my guess about what could be going on with his buckets was correct. Just realizing there is a different possibility of what could be going on to cause someone else's behavior can be enough to save our buckets from feeling invaded and stay in better balance.

Once you grasp that people's actions often stem from their internal bucket levels, you'll start seeing the world through a different lens. It's like suddenly gaining X-ray vision for emotional states! When someone's 'Tough Stuff' bucket is overflowing, it rarely looks like a calm, rational discussion. Instead, you might see them exhibiting:

- **Irritability or Snapping:** Quick tempers, short fuses, or disproportionate reactions to small annoyances. Their Patience Bucket is clearly empty.
- **Withdrawal or Silence:** Pulling away, becoming uncommunicative, or appearing detached. Their Energy or Connection Bucket might be deeply depleted, or their Anxiety Bucket is so full they can't engage.
- **Excessive Complaining or Negativity:** A constant stream of grievances, a pessimistic outlook, or an inability to see any positives. This often indicates an overflowing Frustration or Disappointment Bucket.
- **Overwhelm or Disorganization:** Struggling to focus, missing deadlines, or appearing flustered and chaotic. Their Stress or Tolerance Bucket is likely beyond its limit.
- **Perfectionism or Hyper-control:** An intense need for everything to be 'just so,' coupled with anxiety if it's not. This often points to an overflowing Fear or Anxiety Bucket related to perceived loss of control.

Sometimes, these behaviors are a direct result of recent changes or challenges they're facing – a breakup, a demanding work project, an illness, or something else you might not even be aware they've been dealing with, just like in my volleyball example with my friend. Other times, however, these behaviors are rooted much deeper, stemming from 'rocks' left over from childhood trauma, deeply ingrained subconscious beliefs, or a lifetime of recurring experiences that have filled their 'Tough Stuff' buckets for years. These deeper issues are often much harder for us, as outside observers, to know or understand fully. The deeper issues are also, many times, not even understood by the people being affected by them.

While these observations help you understand others and avoid taking their behavior personally, here's a powerful twist: these are also critical signs to look for in yourself! If you find yourself snapping, withdrawing, complaining excessively, feeling overwhelmed, or becoming overly controlling, consider it a flashing warning light from your own buckets. Just as you learned to identify your own leaks through self-reflection earlier, observing these behaviors in others can sharpen your ability to notice when your own 'Tough Stuff' buckets are nearing their limit. It's an opportunity for a quick internal check-in, allowing you to use those draining strategies we discussed in Chapter 3 before your own buckets spill onto someone else.

Once you recognize that someone else's difficult behavior is a reflection of their overflowing buckets, you gain a superpower: the ability to choose your response rather than automatically reacting. This helps you protect your own precious emotional resources from their 'splash.' However, it's vital to acknowledge that the most effective method often depends on your relationship with that person, and the context of the situation. You wouldn't use the same strategy with your child as you would with your boss or a stranger in a store.

Here are some approaches to consider, keeping your relationship in mind:

- Setting Boundaries: This clearly defines what you will and will not tolerate, and creates space to protect your energy.
  - **With casual acquaintances or difficult strangers:** This might mean physically distancing yourself, ending a conversation politely but firmly, or simply limiting your interactions (e.g., consciously avoiding that overly negative colleague at lunch).

- o **With friends or extended family:** This could involve limiting the duration of calls, steering conversations away from draining topics, or even a direct but kind statement like, 'I care about you, but I'm not able to absorb this level of negativity right now.'
- o **With close family or children:** This becomes about setting emotional boundaries. For a child, it might be, 'I hear you're upset, and I'll talk with you when you can use a calmer voice.' With a partner, it could be agreeing to take a break from an argument before returning with cooler heads. It's managing the interaction, not necessarily avoiding the person.

- **Not Engaging or Disengaging from the Spill (The Emotional Raincoat):** Sometimes, the best response is no response, or to gracefully exit the direct path of the overflow.
  - o **With an irate stranger or a public outburst:** Simply walk away. You don't owe them your emotional energy.
  - o **With an angry boss or a high-stakes professional situation:** Directly confronting an angry boss with empathy might backfire if their bucket is truly overflowing and they're not receptive. Instead, you might use phrases that acknowledge their frustration without taking it on: 'I hear your frustration. Let's schedule a time when we can discuss solutions calmly.' Or, if safe, simply listen without absorbing, letting their words pass by you. I sometimes imagine things like that as if they were a loud car or siren passing by on the road, it might get louder for a bit, but it keeps moving and eventually gets quieter / less disturbing, as shown in Figure 6.
  - o **With a friend or family member:** If they're clearly just venting or spilling without wanting a solution, you might listen for a short, defined period, then gently pivot the conversation, or say, 'I'm sorry you're going through that, but I need to shift to something more positive now.'

- **Active Listening and Empathy (The Compassionate Sponge – Use with Caution!):** In close, trusted relationships, offering empathy can sometimes help them drain their bucket, and strengthen the bond. But this is where caution is key.
  - o **Appropriate use:** When the person is receptive, and you have the emotional capacity, offering a listening ear and validating their feelings ('It sounds like you're really overwhelmed right now') can be incredibly healing for them and deepen your connection. This is a choice you make when your own buckets are balanced enough to offer support without self-depleting.
  - o **When not to use:** If the person consistently uses you as their sole emotional dumping ground without reciprocity, or if your own buckets are running low, trying to be the 'empathetic sponge' will only drain you further.

- **Creating Emotional Distance (The Invisible Shield):** This is a mental strategy that you can use in any situation to prevent external negativity from sticking.
  - o **Whether it's a difficult client,** a critical family member, or someone expressing judgment, you can mentally visualize their words bouncing off an invisible shield around you, racing by you like the sirens on an ambulance as it drives past (Figure 6), or floating away like clouds. Remember the 'lazy river' visualization from Chapter 5? Apply it here: let their tough stuff float past you without clinging. This allows you to acknowledge their existence without letting them fill your buckets.

Figure 6 – Allowing Negative Energy to Pass By Without Affecting You

Navigating Emotional Walls: When Buckets Are Guarded

Sometimes, you might encounter people who seem to have built formidable walls around their buckets (Figure 7). These walls are often erected, consciously or unconsciously, as a protective measure. Perhaps they're trying to keep unvetted tough stuff from getting in and overwhelming them further, or perhaps they're desperately trying to prevent any more good stuff from leaking away after past hurts. These walls can be the legacy of childhood trauma, betrayal, or a lifetime of recurring negative experiences that have taught them to guard their vulnerable emotional core.

When someone has put up these walls, they might not be very receptive to your empathy, no matter how genuine. They might even appear to accept your concern but not truly allow it to facilitate any real change or connection. These walls can manifest as emotional unavailability, resistance to help, or a general closed-off demeanor. It can be incredibly frustrating to encounter these walls when you're genuinely trying to connect or understand.

The Wall Protects... And Isolates

Figure 7 – When a Wall is Put up to Protect Buckets

It's often easier to spot when others have put up walls than it is to see them in ourselves. If you find yourself consistently feeling emotionally disconnected, unwilling to let others in, or struggling to accept help even when you need it, that's a signal to look inward.

Are you building walls around your own buckets? Recognizing these tendencies in yourself is another powerful point of self-reflection, allowing you to gently explore whether those walls are still serving you or if they're now preventing essential good stuff from getting in or tough stuff from getting out.

These deep-seated walls, rooted in subconscious patterns, can be incredibly difficult to dismantle on your own. In fact, many individuals I've worked with tell me they've been through years of traditional therapy methods, diligently working to understand and chip away at these barriers, often with limited success. This is precisely where approaches like hypnotherapy shine. Some of my most fulfilling experiences as a hypnotherapist have been hearing clients tell me they couldn't 'crack that wall' despite years of effort, yet in just a few hypnotherapy sessions, they not only gain a profound understanding of its origins, but can actually feel it coming down (that's right, "…when the walls come tumblin' down, when the walls come crumblin' crumblin', when the walls come tumblin' tumblin' dooowwwwn…", shout out to John Mellancamp for that 80s banger). They start to see a future without that impenetrable barrier, or at least one where the 'wall' has transformed into more of a 'fence with a gate' – something they can manage and choose to open when it serves them, rather than being trapped behind it.

The Drain of Assumption and Judgment: Observing vs. Labeling

As we've just discussed, trying to understand what's truly driving someone else's behavior can be incredibly complex. Sometimes, their actions are clearly linked to recent events we know about. Other times, they're rooted in deep-seated 'rocks' or long-standing 'walls' that are entirely invisible to us. And this brings us to a significant way we often, unknowingly, drain our own buckets: by assuming we know the 'why' behind someone else's actions, and then judging them for it.

When we see someone behaving in a way we don't understand or agree with, our minds often rush to fill in the blanks. We create narratives, assign motives, and label their actions as 'lazy,' 'selfish,' 'rude,' or 'incompetent.' But here's the kicker: these assumptions and judgments are almost always based on incomplete information filtered through the unique lens of our own buckets and past experiences. Every time you construct a negative judgment about someone else, you're essentially filling your own Frustration or Anger Bucket with tough stuff that doesn't actually serve you. It's a self-inflicted drain.

This is where it's vital to distinguish between judging and simply observing.

- Judging is attaching a positive or negative label, often with moral weight, to a person or their behavior. It implies a definitive understanding of their motives, character, or the entirety of their situation. For example: 'They are so inconsiderate for being late.' or 'They're just lazy and don't care.'
- Observing, on the other hand, is simply noticing facts without immediately evaluating or categorizing them, as demonstrated in Figure 8. It's seeing what is happening, without layering on your interpretation of why it's happening or what it means about them as a person. For example: 'They arrived thirty minutes after the agreed time.' or 'They haven't completed the task yet.'

Figure 8 – Observation vs Judgment

We tend to judge much more than we realize because our brains are wired to make sense of the world, and our own buckets, filled with our unique history, beliefs, and values, are constantly influencing how we perceive everything. What seems perfectly reasonable to you might seem completely baffling to someone else, and vice-versa. Your overflowing Patience Bucket might lead you to calmly observe a slow cashier, while someone with a nearly empty one might immediately judge them as 'incompetent.'

By learning to pause before judging and consciously shifting to mere observation, you stop the insidious drain that judgment causes. You acknowledge the external reality without allowing it to automatically generate negative emotions within your own system. It doesn't mean you condone harmful behavior, but it does mean you protect your own inner peace by choosing not to take on the burden of their perceived flaws.

Practice Makes (More) Peaceful: An Exercise in Observation
Learning to observe without judging is a muscle that strengthens with consistent use. It won't happen overnight, but every conscious effort you make will save your own buckets from unnecessary splashes of tough stuff.

Here's a simple exercise you can practice throughout your day:

The 'Bucket-Watcher' Exercise:

1. **Choose Your Subject (Carefully!):** Start small. Pick a person or a situation where you often find yourself forming quick judgments, but where the stakes are relatively low. This could be someone in traffic, a celebrity you see on the news, a character in a TV show, or a casual acquaintance. Avoid practicing this first on someone with whom you have a highly charged or difficult relationship, as that requires more developed skills.

2. **Notice the Behavior (Observe, Observe, Observe):** Simply become aware of what they are doing or saying without adding any immediate interpretation.
    o   *Instead of:* "That person is so rude."
        Try: "That person just pushed past someone without making eye contact."
    o   *Instead of:* "They're clearly trying to get attention."
        Try: "They are speaking loudly and gesturing expressively."

3. **Catch the Judgment (Your Inner Critic):** As you observe, notice when your mind automatically jumps to a judgment. Don't criticize yourself for judging – it's a deeply ingrained habit. Just acknowledge the thought: "Ah, there's my judgment trying to label them."

4. **Reframe to Observation (The Neutral Lens):** Consciously rephrase your judgmental thought into a purely factual, neutral observation.
    o   *If your thought was:* "They're so lazy."
        Reframe to: "They haven't started that task yet."
    o   *If your thought was:* "That's a ridiculous outfit."
        Reframe to: "That person is wearing bright colors and unconventional patterns."

5. **Connect to a Potential Bucket State (Hypothesize, Don't Conclude):** Briefly consider what their bucket might be experiencing that could lead to that behavior, without needing to be right.
   o   "Maybe their Stress Bucket is overflowing."
   o   "Perhaps their Joy Bucket is full, and they're just expressing themselves freely."
   o   "Could their Patience Bucket be running on empty?"

6. **Notice Your Own Bucket:** As you practice this shift from judgment to observation, pay attention to what happens inside your own buckets. Do you feel less agitated? Less invested in being 'right'? More at peace? Often, the very act of withholding judgment prevents your own Frustration or Anger Buckets from filling unnecessarily. I know for me, personally, this was a game changer. I didn't realize how much I was judging and how much it filled my Frustration Bucket and drained my Patience Bucket. I can't say I'm perfect at avoiding judgment now, but man do I feel so much lighter and more in control of my responses having added this tool to my toolbox!

This exercise is not intended to make you more robotic, or to condone behavior that causes harm. Instead, it's consciously choosing to loosen the grip of automatic judgment, thereby reducing the internal tough stuff you experience. It's a powerful act of self-preservation and compassion, for both yourself and for others. You might also want to keep in mind what the primary Love Language is for someone else you care about and, if they are struggling with overflowing or empty buckets, use the Language that will be more effective in bringing their buckets back to healthier levels as you interact with them.

I must admit, growing up in a non-smoking family, I used to be pretty judgmental towards smokers. Heck, with all the commercials trying to scare people out of smoking, it was hard to NOT judge the people who smoked anyway. However, I now truly see smokers as people who most likely have a different size Stress Bucket (or one that's filled with rocks), and at some point it just worked out in their minds that smoking cigarettes seemed to make that bucket feel more stable. Based on some of my clients' stories of what they've lived through, their bucket might actually be much bigger than mine to even hold some of their heavy rocks that might not even fit in one of my buckets. I've used this metaphor with many clients who judge themselves pretty harshly for smoking, and it really helps them take their foot off the self-blame petal and puts a little extra hope in their 'Good Stuff' buckets.

As we strive to understand others' bucket systems and cultivate compassion, it becomes clear that there's an incredible, beautiful diversity in how our emotional containers are built and filled. It's about so much more than the fundamental buckets like joy or stress; it extends to more specialized capacities that truly define our individual preferences and personalities.

Take, for instance, your Humor Bucket. Just like your Stress or Patience Buckets, your Humor Bucket has its own unique size and preferred 'fills.' Think about it: have you ever shared a joke that you found absolutely hilarious, only to be met with blank stares or polite chuckles? Or perhaps someone else's idea of a good laugh just leaves you scratching your head? That's your Humor Bucket at play! For some, their Humor Bucket might be a vibrant, overflowing magenta, easily filled by slapstick comedy and puns. For others, it might be a subtle, deep indigo, requiring dry wit or intellectual humor to get even a trickle. The 'fills' for this bucket are incredibly personal – what one person finds hysterical, another might find completely unfunny, or even offensive. This is why we have so many different types of comedy and so many different reactions! Understanding that each person's Humor Bucket has a unique 'color' or preference helps us appreciate individual differences, avoid offense, and simply acknowledge that not everyone finds the same things funny, and that's perfectly okay. It's just another beautiful aspect of our unique Emotional Bucket Balancing Systems.

Similarly, consider someone's Adventure Bucket. We all have varying capacities for seeking thrills, trying new things, or stepping outside our comfort zones. I know some adrenaline junkies who always seem to be pushing the limits of safety, like their Adventure Buckets have infinite capacity – think skydivers, cliff divers, or free divers. Kudos to them for living their lives large, fully embracing their unique thresholds for excitement! But then, we may realize some of our own buckets, like our Adventure Bucket, are simply smaller than someone else's, and we are completely okay with that. I have no interest in doing most of those extreme things. And I'm not entirely averse to adventure! I've ziplined on the side of a volcano (it wasn't erupting at the time), gone white water rafting, snorkeled in the ocean, and I've even sung a solo in front of over 200 people, most of whom I didn't know (and my only 'training' for that was high school choir a couple decades earlier and singing in the car to myself since then). That was certainly putting myself out there! Of course there's also those who might have a much smaller Adventure Bucket, who wouldn't be interested in even travelling to another country or going on a cruise ship. With someone like that you need to understand that a surprise trip to Mexico is not likely to be received well and could explode one or more of their buckets.

It's incredibly helpful to realize that the diversity in our various bucket systems—whether it's for humor, adventure, or anything else—is not only okay, but a fundamental part of what makes each of us unique, and what makes human connection so interesting. We don't have to try to make our Adventure Bucket the same size as an extreme athlete's, nor should we judge someone whose Patience Bucket is smaller than our own. Recognizing and respecting these individual differences fosters true acceptance and deepens our compassion for both ourselves and everyone around us.

Mastering your own emotional bucket balancing system is the bedrock of well-being. Understanding others' buckets, letting go of judgment, and protecting your own from unnecessary splashes are powerful extensions of that mastery. You're building a truly robust emotional foundation and stepping into the natural FLOWS of life.

But how do you ensure these practices become second nature? How do you keep your buckets optimally managed, not just in moments of crisis, but consistently, as a way of life? This is where we move from understanding and repairing to sustaining and thriving. In Chapter 7: Thriving in the Flow: Sustaining Your Optimized Buckets, we'll explore how to integrate these tools into your daily rhythm, creating habits that ensure your emotional well-being flows effortlessly, even when life inevitably throws new challenges your way.

"When you listen with empathy to another person, you give that person psychological air."
- Stephen R. Covey

Chapter 7 Thriving in the Flow: Sustaining Your Optimized Buckets

You've embarked on an incredible journey through your emotional landscape, learning to mind your own buckets and even gain a deeper understanding of others'. But knowing all of this useful information is one thing; consistently applying it and truly navigating the EBBS and FLOWS of life is another. This chapter is about taking all those insights and integrating them into your daily rhythm, ensuring your emotional well-being isn't just a fleeting good day, but a sustained way of being.

One of the most immediate and delightful ways to put your newfound 'bucket literacy' into practice is to use it as a powerful communication tool. Think about it: how often do you struggle to articulate that you're feeling overwhelmed, frustrated, or simply running on empty without sounding whiny, blame-y, or just plain stressed? The bucket metaphor offers a playful, non-confrontational, and incredibly clear way to signal your emotional state to others, allowing them to respond with more understanding and less guesswork.

Instead of saying, 'You're really annoying me right now!' (which could immediately fill their self-defense/fight-back bucket!), you can playfully state, 'Please don't do that right now, my Patience Bucket is almost completely empty!'

This simple shift changes everything. It externalizes the emotion, making it about a 'bucket' rather than a personal failing or accusation. It's disarming and often invites empathy because it paints such a vivid, relatable picture.

Consider how you could use it in different scenarios:

- When you're overwhelmed: Instead of 'I can't handle anything else,' try, 'My Stress Bucket is overflowing, so I really need a quiet evening tonight.'
- When you're physically tired: Instead of 'I'm exhausted, leave me alone,' you might say, 'My Energy Bucket is running on fumes – can we tackle that later?'
- When you're trying to set a boundary: Instead of 'I don't like when you complain so much,' try, 'My Optimism Bucket is getting really drained by this conversation.'
- When you need help refilling a bucket that is running dry for you: Instead of 'I feel completely hopeless and ready to give up,' try 'My Hope Bucket is leaking pretty bad, can you remind me of some challenges I've overcome so I can start patching that up?'
- And for the good stuff too! Instead of just a general 'I'm happy,' you could share, 'My Joy Bucket is absolutely brimming today!' or 'My Connection Bucket feels so full after our chat!'

Not only does this type of communication help you express your needs more clearly, but it also subtly educates those around you. When you start using 'bucket language,' you might be surprised how quickly others pick it up. Imagine a world where your loved ones could gently tell you, 'Hey, your Anxiety Bucket seems pretty full, can I help drain some of that?' or 'My Compassion Bucket could use a refill today.' This shared language fosters greater empathy and allows everyone to better support each other's emotional well-being, contributing to a much smoother, more sustainable 'flow' in your relationships and daily life. On top of having a new shared language in your relationships, consider gauging your expectations of those you are in close relationships with by acknowledging what you learn about their bucket capacities so you can better avoid pushing their buttons and causing unnecessary drama.

Anticipating and Preparing for Challenges: Your Emotional Weather Forecast

Life, by its very nature, is a series of ups and downs. No matter how adept you become at managing your buckets, there will always be unexpected downpours, sudden gales, and periods where the tough stuff seems to come at you in waves. The goal isn't to avoid these challenges – that's impossible – but rather to become a skilled emotional meteorologist, able to anticipate potential storms and prepare your bucket system to weather them with resilience.

Think of it like preparing for a significant weather event. You wouldn't wait for a hurricane to hit before boarding up your windows and stocking your pantry, right? The same proactive mindset applies to your emotional health. By anticipating challenges, you empower yourself to reinforce your buckets before the pressure hits, turning potential crises into manageable moments.

How to Become Your Own Emotional Meteorologist:

1. **Know Your Personal Weather Patterns (Self-Awareness):** You've already done a lot of work on identifying your own leaks and triggers in Chapter 5. This is where that deep self-awareness really pays off. What events, situations, or types of people reliably tend to fill your Stress, Anxiety, or Frustration Buckets? Do holidays often deplete your Patience Bucket? Does a busy work day always leave your Energy Bucket running on fumes? Learning from your past reactions is your most powerful forecasting tool.

2. **Scan the Horizon (Forecasting Upcoming Events):** Look ahead in your calendar or simply consider your upcoming life events. Are there:
   o   Major deadlines or projects at work?
   o   Upcoming family gatherings (especially those with complex dynamics)?
   o   Travel plans, even if fun, that can be inherently draining?
   o   Holidays or anniversaries that carry emotional weight?
   o   Significant personal appointments (doctor, dentist, taxes)?

o   Periods of increased social demands?

Identify these potential 'high-pressure systems' for your emotional buckets.

3. **Proactive Bucket Management (Pre-Storm Preparations):** Once you've identified a potential challenge, you can strategically prepare your buckets. You won't need to avoid the event entirely, but consciously strengthen your capacity to navigate it:
    o   **Pre-Fill Your 'Good Stuff' Buckets:** In the days or weeks leading up to the anticipated challenge, intentionally pour extra good stuff into your key buckets. If you know a stressful work week is coming, consciously prioritize activities that fill your Joy and Peace Buckets: schedule extra time for hobbies, connect with uplifting friends, spend time in nature, or engage in your favorite self-care rituals. You're essentially building up reserves.
    o   **Pre-Drain Your 'Tough Stuff' Buckets:** Don't wait for the overwhelm to hit. Actively use your draining strategies (from Chapter 3) to clear out any existing stress or anxiety. Get extra exercise, meditate more frequently, journal out any nagging worries, or engage in your preferred physical release methods. Create as much empty space as possible in those 'Tough Stuff' buckets beforehand.
    o   **Pre-Plug Known Leaks:** Reinforce those boundaries you've learned to set. Say 'no' to extra commitments that would stretch you too thin. Delegate tasks where possible. Ensure your sleep and nutrition (basic needs, Chapter 2) are absolutely on point. Don't let small, controllable leaks weaken your system when a larger storm is approaching.
    o   **Have a 'Go-To' Emergency Kit:** Know what quick fill or drain strategies work best and fastest for you. Keep them readily accessible. This might be a favorite song, a short breathing exercise, a five-minute walk outside, or a quick

call to a supportive friend. A critical caution here: make sure these 'go-to' solutions are genuinely healthy for you in the long run. Relying too heavily on behaviors like smoking, excessive alcohol consumption, or overeating, for instance, might offer temporary distraction, but they often act as subtle leaks or create larger problems for your buckets down the line. Choose tools that truly replenish and support you, rather than those that come back to haunt you.

By approaching life's challenges with this proactive, anticipatory mindset, you transform yourself from being a victim of circumstance to a confident captain of your own emotional ship. You're not just hoping for calm seas; you're ensuring your vessel is sturdy and your crew (your internal resources) are ready for whatever the emotional weather forecast brings.

Consistency is Key: The Power of Daily Habits
You've learned to forecast emotional storms and even prepare your buckets for the big ones. But just as a healthy body isn't built on occasional crash diets or intense workouts once a month, a thriving emotional bucket balancing system isn't sustained by grand, infrequent gestures. True, effortless 'FLOWS' come from the quiet, consistent power of daily habits.

Think of your emotional buckets like your physical health: you brush your teeth every day to prevent cavities, not just when you get one. You eat nourishing meals consistently, not just when you're facing a nutritional deficiency. Emotional well-being works the same way. It's about shifting from crisis management to continuous, proactive maintenance. This doesn't necessarily mean adding hours of self-care to your already busy day, but weaving small, intentional acts of bucket management into the fabric of your life.

These are your 'micro-maintenance' moments:

- **Mini Check-Ins:** Take a few moments each day to simply ask yourself, 'Which of my buckets feels full right now? Which feels a bit low? Is there any overflow or a sneaky leak I'm noticing?' This quick self-scan takes mere seconds but builds powerful self-awareness.
- **Micro-Fills:** What small things bring you a burst of good stuff? It might be listening to one favorite song, looking at a cherished photo, taking three deep, appreciative breaths, or simply savoring a sip of water. Don't wait until your Joy Bucket is empty to add a drop; consistent micro-fills can keep it topped up and resilient.
- **Micro-Drains:** Equally important are the tiny releases of 'tough stuff.' Instead of letting minor frustrations accumulate, practice a quick micro-drain. This could be a sigh, a shoulder roll, stepping away from your screen for 60 seconds, or mentally 'tossing' a small worry into an imaginary drain or a bonfire. These small acts prevent those trickles of stress from becoming a torrent.
- **Brief Boundary Reviews:** Take a moment to mentally review your boundaries. Did you uphold them today? Was there a moment you needed to say no and didn't? This quick mental reinforcement helps plug leaks before they become significant drains. Don't beat yourself up if you had some misses, this is just a practice in becoming more self-aware. And remember, if you struggle to be able to identify these things in yourself, check-in with a trusted friend or family member until you get better at self-assessment.
- **Heart-Focused Breathing (Mini Sessions):** You learned this powerful technique in Chapter 2. You don't need a twenty-minute meditation session to benefit. Even 60-90 seconds of focused, heart-centered breathing can recalibrate your system, generate positive emotion, and prevent your Stress Bucket from rising.

The beauty of consistency in these small actions is that it prevents major overflows, builds emotional resilience, and makes your entire bucket system feel increasingly effortless and fluid. You're not just reacting to life; you're flowing with it, maintaining balance day in and day out.

Celebrating Small Wins: Fueling Your Flow

In our drive to achieve big goals and tackle major challenges, we often overlook the most powerful fuel for sustained motivation and well-being: the small wins. These are the quiet, internal victories in your daily battle to maintain emotional flow. Learning to recognize these moments is important because they directly affect your day, filling your 'Good Stuff' buckets and reinforcing positive behaviors.

So, what do these 'small wins' in bucket management actually look like? They are often moments of subtle but profound internal shifts or conscious choices that steer your emotional system in a healthier direction:

- You recognized a rising tide: You noticed your Stress Bucket starting to fill before it overflowed, or felt your Patience Bucket nearing empty, and you chose to take a breath, step away, or acknowledge the feeling.
- You communicated with 'bucket language': You successfully used a phrase like, 'My Frustration Bucket is getting pretty full, so I need to step away for a moment,' and the other person understood (or at least, you didn't escalate the situation!).
- You chose observation over judgment: You caught yourself about to label someone, and instead, you consciously reframed your thought to a neutral observation, as practiced in the previous chapter.
- You deployed a micro-fill or micro-drain: You intentionally paused to listen to a favorite song for 60 seconds, took a few heart-focused breaths, or mentally tossed a small worry into an imaginary drain, and felt a subtle shift.
- You upheld a boundary: You said 'no' to an extra commitment, declined a draining conversation, or created space for yourself when you needed it, even if it felt a little uncomfortable.

- You broke a pattern: You typically react with anger to a specific trigger, but this time, you paused, used a strategy, and responded differently.

How do these seemingly small moments affect your day? Their impact is far from small:

- Immediate 'Good Stuff' Fillers: Each small win immediately pours a bit of Achievement, Confidence, Self-Efficacy, or Hope into your corresponding 'Good Stuff' buckets. This provides an instant boost, making you feel more capable and in control.
- Preventative Power: By addressing the small trickles of tough stuff or reinforcing good habits, you prevent larger emotional overflows later in the day. This saves you from significant energy drains and allows your good stuff to remain dominant.
- Builds Momentum: Every acknowledged small win acts like a mental 'high-five,' reinforcing the positive behavior. It makes you more likely to repeat the action, building a stronger habit loop. This creates an upward spiral where one good choice makes the next one easier.
- Shifts Focus: Instead of solely focusing on problems or what went wrong, recognizing small wins trains your brain to look for progress, resilience, and opportunities for growth. This positive focus alone can significantly improve your overall mood and outlook.

The Reinforcing Feedback Loop: Building Effortless Flow

You've now gathered an impressive arsenal of tools for understanding, managing, and proactively preparing your emotional buckets to better experience the Freedom, Lightness, Openness, Wellness, and Serenity (FLOWS) of life. But here's the truly powerful secret that underpins sustained well-being: your bucket system isn't a static set of rules; it's a dynamic, self-reinforcing loop. Every conscious choice you make, every small act of bucket management, doesn't just address the immediate moment – it strengthens the entire system, making future efforts easier and more effective.

Think of it this way:

- Each Positive Action Makes the Next Action Easier: When you successfully observe without judging, or when you consciously implement a micro-drain, you don't just clear out a little tough stuff; you also build a pathway in your brain. That momentary success fills your Confidence Bucket and makes it slightly easier to choose that same positive action next time. Instead of feeling defeated by an overflowing bucket, you feel competent and capable, providing you with more emotional energy to apply to the next situation.
- The Compounding Effect: Small Efforts Yield Massive Shifts Over Time: Just like compound interest in finance, the consistent, small efforts you make with your buckets accumulate into significant, often profound, shifts in your overall emotional landscape. A single daily micro-fill or a conscious reframe of a judgmental thought might seem insignificant on its own. But practice these consistently over weeks, months, and years, and you'll find your baseline emotional state becomes lighter, more resilient, and far less susceptible to deep drains or overwhelming spills. You're not just managing moments; you're fundamentally reshaping your emotional capacity and reactivity.
- Increased Control and Agency: From Puppet to Puppet Master: This consistent engagement with your bucket system cultivates a profound sense of control and empowerment. You move from feeling like a passive recipient of whatever life throws at you to an active participant, capable of influencing your internal state. You learn that while you can't always control the 'rain' outside, you absolutely can manage your inner 'drainage system' and reinforce your emotional infrastructure. This empowered feeling, in itself, becomes a potent filler for your Confidence and Peace Buckets.

This is the essence of thriving in the flow. You'll still have tough stuff entering your buckets from time to time. But now you're reaching a point where the processes of recognizing, managing, draining, filling, and protecting your buckets become so integrated into your daily reality that they feel effortless. You're attuned to your emotional weather, you have your tools ready, and you've built a robust, responsive system that allows you to navigate life's inevitable currents with grace, resilience, and a consistent sense of inner peace. You are not just reacting to the flow; you are confidently flowing with it, and that makes navigating life feel so much easier!

Chapter 8 Setting the High Score for BBR, Bucket Breakthrough Revolution

Whew! You've navigated the levels, dodged the obstacles, and mastered new moves in the game of emotional well-being. Take a moment, high-five yourself, or maybe even do a little victory dance (perhaps a throwback to Dance Dance Revolution (DDR) for you PlayStation fans... I LOVED that game). You've journeyed behind the emotional curtain, bravely explored your inner bucket system, and emerged not just with knowledge, but with a powerful new strategy guide for life. Give yourself a moment to truly appreciate what you've accomplished – you're well on your way to setting the high score for your own BBR (Bucket Breakthrough Revolution)!

Remember when spilling a coffee could derail your entire day, or when you felt like a slave to your own overwhelming emotions? That was then. Now, you understand your unique collection and capacities of emotional buckets – what fills your Joy and Patience Buckets, what drains your Stress and Anxiety, and how those sneaky leaks and stubborn rocks have been impacting your flow. You've learned to be your own emotional meteorologist, anticipating challenges and preparing your system, rather than being swept away by every storm. You've discovered how to speak 'bucket language' to others, setting boundaries and inviting compassion with a touch of playful clarity. Most powerfully, you've embraced the art of observing without judging, protecting your own precious energy from unnecessary emotional splashes.

While this doesn't put you in a persistent state of perpetual bliss, it does help you gain control, cultivate resilience, and live with greater compassion – both for yourself and for those around you. You've built a robust, responsive system that allows you to confidently navigate life's currents, ensuring your good stuff flows freely and your tough stuff finds its proper drain. You're no longer just reacting; you're flowing with life. If you've ever stood even knee deep in the ocean with the waves coming in, you know it's much harder to try and stop a wave (or even stand still while it hits) than to go with the wave and let it push you back onto the beach. If you haven't experienced something like that, let me tell you, it's much easier and more enjoyable to ride the wave instead of trying to stand up to one (to be clear, I never conquered actually standing up on a surf board, but I've loved boogie boarding and body surfing).

It is important to recognize that this bucket metaphor is flexible and can be interpreted differently based on the person or situation. For example, in some cases having an empty Stress Bucket might seem desirable, and a full or overflowing one signifies a problem, on the other hand, some might see it more as an empty Stress Bucket means there are no resources left to handle more Stress, therefore that is the case that needs some tending. Consider the Patience Bucket. If a person states their Patience Bucket is empty, this might be understood to mean they possess no patience left to give. Conversely, if they say their Patience Bucket is overflowing or full, this could suggest they have reached a state of maximum tolerance and have no more room to handle frustrating situations. Typically, the context of how someone is referring to their buckets will clue you in on whether they feel it's a good or bad state. If they interpret the state of their bucket different than you, that's another opportunity for you to practice Observation instead of Judgment because telling them they are wrong about their bucket experience is not likely to be helpful.

The work, of course, doesn't stop here. It's not a one-and-done magic trick, but a lifelong practice. The more you 'Mind Your Buckets' – consistently checking in, celebrating those small wins, and consciously choosing your responses – the more effortless and intuitive it will become. It's like building emotional muscle memory, where the healthy habits become your default, automatically steering you towards balance and well-being.

So, as we bring this book to a close, remember: you've got the tools. You've got the understanding. You've got the power. Go forth, be the master of your emotional flow, and as my favorite a capella group, Pentatonix, likes to sing about empowerment and hope, '…hear me when I say, it's time to celebrate, like New Years Day!' You are ready to thrive!

Keep an eye out for additional versions of this book to be released in the future, targeted at more specific audiences to make it even more easily relatable to additional groups of people (kids, teens, managers, etc.). We're also working on creating a workbook, or mobile app, to help you navigate your personal EBBS and FLOWS more specifically. There is also something to be said for extending this metaphor beyond emotional buckets, applying the concept to things like abilities to reason, physical abilities (e.g., some people are natural athletes, others, not so much), artistic talents (I'm consistently amazed at how some people can play an instrument and sing at the same time), etc. In the meantime, just being aware that there's even more to this metaphor that can be helpful to consider to help make life easier to understand might allow you to figure some things out on your own.

If you're eager to dive even deeper, to get more personalized support in truly integrating these concepts into your daily reality, or to explore specific techniques for shifting those stubborn 'rocks' and optimizing your flow through the power of your subconscious mind, know that there are resources available. My courses and specialized hypnotic recordings are designed to provide that extra guidance, helping you embed these profound changes on an even deeper level.

I'm so grateful that you felt intrigued enough to read this book. I encourage you to seize this opportunity and begin your new chapter! Connect today to continue your journey toward truly effortless emotional well-being. For more on those resources, go to mindyourbuckets.com. Or, of course, if you're looking for more individualized, in-person support, seek out a therapist, life coach or hypnotherapist in your area.

About the Author

 Hey there! I hope you've enjoyed this book and truly feel better equipped to handle some of life's challenges now. So, who am I and why did I write this book about buckets? Well, let me tell you a little bit about my journey.

I grew up in a small town called Wilmington, in southwest Ohio, smack dab in the middle, between Cincinnati and Columbus. School was pretty easy for me – always pulled good grades. And sports? Yep, I was all in, especially with volleyball, running the team as a starting setter in high school, and on club teams in the off season, and even playing 3 years as a defensive specialist and backup setter (I'm 5'6" on a good day... not a height that really lends itself to much success in the front row) at a small NCAA Division 1 school, Wright State University, in Dayton, Ohio.

When I first started college, I thought I'd be an accountant. Made sense at the time. I knew I was good at math, and my first ever boss said I was super meticulous (the job was picking strawberries in the summer back in middle school). But then, part way through my freshman year, a volleyball teammate changed everything. She was in the Human Factors Engineering program (which I'd never heard of before), and when she explained it – designing stuff like products, systems, and processes to be easier, more efficient, and safer for people to use – my brain just lit up! That sounded way more interesting than reporting numbers. I was also pretty interested in Human Factors Psychology, but I was told getting a decent job in that field usually meant getting a PhD, and I was ready to get out there in the real world to start making my own money and my own life with a bachelor's in engineering.

A couple of years after college, I landed a cool job as a Human Factors Engineer at GE in Melbourne, Florida. I got to hang out with train dispatchers (yep, real ones!) and help design a totally new system for them to manage train traffic. It was fascinating to see the everyday struggles our users had and then figure out how to make their lives easier, and the railroads safer, with our new system.

After about five or six years, though, I realized working for a giant corporation like GE just wasn't really me. I mean, when I started, it was a smaller joint venture, so it felt pretty close-knit, but once GE bought out the other company, it definitely wasn't small anymore! I tried going out on my own as an ergonomics entrepreneur for a bit, but honestly, I didn't have a clue how to build a business back then. So, I ended up at Harris Corporation, again doing Human Factors and Systems Engineering applied to software design, for almost ten years before making a huge jump and starting my own hypnotherapy practice.

That decision didn't come out of the blue, there were actually three big things that pushed me to take the leap:

First, I read this incredible book called The Journey by Brandon Bays. She talked about how she actually cured her own cancer by digging into some old emotional stuff, and it literally blew my mind – like, her body healed itself! Then I went to a weekend workshop to learn more about the techniques she used and realized, 'Holy cow, I could actually help people do this!'

Second, I had my own experience with hypnotherapy. I wasn't even sure I could be hypnotized, especially knowing how analytical I was as an engineer, but it worked! And it worked really well. It was also intriguing that the hypnotherapist I went to had left her practice as a medical doctor because she felt hypnotherapy was healing the root of people's problems instead of feeling like she was just prescribing meds that only tried to erase the symptom, not the root cause.

And third, I was working with a personal trainer who had an inspiring vision for a holistic healing community. As we talked about his plans, I realized that kind of work was way, way more exciting than what I was doing at my corporate job (designing back-office software user interfaces, which might make someone more efficient at their job, but wasn't exactly life-altering). When I told him that, he asked what I'd truly be passionate about, and those ideas from The Journey workshop instantly popped into my head. But now, after my own hypnotherapy experience, I knew that was basically the same concept, just more established, and I could get a recognized certification to feel more prepared and capable of helping people transform their lives.

So, I found an awesome licensed hypnotherapy school in Tampa, Florida, that allowed me the flexibility to keep working while I trained. After 500 hours and three certifications, I completed that schooling in October 2013 and officially left Harris in February 2014 to jump into my practice full-time. Do I miss the engineering job? Well, I definitely miss the friendships and the comfy salary and benefits. But honestly, working with clients and helping them through some truly amazing (and sometimes challenging) transitions? That's brought me so much more fulfillment.

Since then, I've also dived into HeartMath and Emotional Intelligence training. These tools have been absolute game-changers, not just for my clients but in my own life too. And through all those thousands of client sessions, I've noticed some things and developed these powerful metaphors that really click for people and help them feel better. The bucket analogy has been one of the most impactful ones, hands down. That's why I just had to share it with a broader audience in a book – to spread that positive impact as wide as possible!

It's crazy how we don't get taught stuff like this in school, right? But these concepts are so powerful! They can make such huge shifts in how we interact with ourselves and each other, making those interactions more effective, efficient, and safe. And you know what? That's been the common thread through both of my seemingly totally different careers. It all comes back to helping humans connect and function better! I hope this book helps achieve that, creating a positive ripple effect that reaches far and wide.

As I mentioned earlier in the book, the name I chose for my business, once I knew I wanted it to appeal to more than just people specifically seeking out hypnotherapy, was EPIC Renewal, where EPIC stands for External Peace, Internal Calm. It has always been my goal in life to help people renew that sense of peace and getting along with each other, as well as calming the struggles they encounter within themselves. I'm so grateful that I get the opportunity to do that each day with my clients, and now, with this book, extending that reach even further! If you find this book helpful, share your experience with others! Write a review, tell friends and family, share your book with someone else you think could benefit from these concepts. Together, we can make an EPIC positive shift in our society!

Acknowledgments

I truly want to thank everyone who encouraged and supported me in writing this book. First, I am very appreciative that I had a family and community growing up that was positive and encouraging. I'm not sure I would have had the drive on my own if those around me were consistently doubting me and tearing me down. I also want to thank my personal trainer (from the 2012 time frame), Terrance, for encouraging me to pursue my passion, if not for him I would probably still be at a desk job, frustrated with the feeling of not having a real impact in a large corporation. And I certainly want to thank my partner in life, Jason, for being understanding and supportive throughout this process.

I'm also appreciative of the concepts and mindsets that Unity of Melbourne and the Institute of Interpersonal Hypnotherapy (formerly The Florida Institute of Hypnotherapy) exposed me to, which helped me develop into the person (and hypnotherapist) that I am today.

In addition to several clients that I initially mentioned the idea of writing this book to (after explaining the bucket metaphor to them), I've also had several good friends and family who were very encouraging, including Karine and Chantelle, who were the first to actually read the entire first draft, giving rave reviews, which reenforced for me that this book could have great positive impacts for people beyond my clients! I need to also thank friend and colleague, Deidre Beacham, for her support and guidance in working through the process of getting the book published. Her experience and knowledge has been profoundly helpful and took the pressure off me trying to navigate the whole process on my own.

The images throughout this book, other than the headshot in the About the Author section, were generated with the help of Gemini AI. Gemini AI was also used to help generate the content of the book. I struggled for a bit on how to even start writing about this metaphor, but the prompts it came up with were very helpful in getting over that writer's block and making it a more interesting read. If you are considering writing a book, but don't have an expert in your pocket and aren't sure how to start, I highly recommend chatting with an AI interface about what your book would be about, who you would be writing it for (expected audience), and let it guide you with prompts and questions that I know made this process much quicker and easier for me.

If you believe you have a book in you, I strongly encourage you to do your best to get it out there... you never know who needs to hear your story and the ripple effect it can have!

Additional Resources

These resources have either been referenced within the content of this book, were part of the inspiration in writing it, or can give even more detailed information that can be helpful in Minding Your Buckets!

Books:
- The Four Agreements, by Don Miguel Ruiz
- The Five Love Languages, by Gary Chapman
- The Big Leap, by Gay Hendricks
- Completely Connected, by Rita Marie Johnson
- The Journey, by Brandon Bays

Websites:
- Mindyourbuckets.com
- Hypnohuddle.com
- HeartMath.com and HeartMath.org
- Connectionpractice.org
- Empowerma.com

I encourage you to seek out positive, encouraging songs, poems, or other writings as options to be used in times when you need something to help fill your 'Good Stuff' buckets when they are running low. Empower Music and Arts is an organization that promotes Posi artists, so if you aren't finding it elsewhere, their website (listed above) is a good place to try.

www.ingramcontent.com/pod-product-compliance
Lightning Source LLC
Chambersburg PA
CBHW020326290526
45785CB00007B/2931